Alfalfa*bit*
Soup

by Gail Swanson

CHAMBERS PUBLISHING GROUP
CLEVELAND, OH
1998

Published in the Western Hemisphere by

Underwood Imprint of
Chambers Publishing Group
18515 Underwood Avenue
Cleveland,OH 44119   USA
1-800-910-1195

"Although *Alfalfabit Soup* is based on many actual events, the
characters in this book are fictitious. Any resemblance to
persons living or dead is coincidental."

10987654321

ISBN No. 1-892509-14-8

Cover Art/Design:
Eric Antonik
antonik@apk.net

Text Styling:
Abram Ross, Inc.
1046 Literary St.
Cleveland, OH 44113
http://www.abramross.com

DEDICATION

This book is dedicated to "Ludwig and Pu" and to all the hard-working folk who put food on our tables.

Alfalabit Soup

Chapter One

Life: Subject to Change Without Notice

Five years ago we belonged to a country club. Today we are the Country Club. We do not charge membership, but we do accept sweat-of-the-brow credit.

We belong to an elite group of people who work from dawn til dawn, come rain or shine, hell or high water. We are not disgruntled postal workers. We are farmers.

This former fashion model traded her designer labels for a pair of insulated Carhartt overalls. Flying around in our red convertible sports car is no longer an option. My husband traded our mid-life crisis vehicle for a brown pickup truck.

The decision to chuck the city life did not happen overnight. People often ask me if I always wanted to live on a farm. City folks wonder how I could leave the "good life behind."

Growing up, I really didn't give much thought to soybeans or alfalfa. I wanted a penguin. My plan was to keep him in the refrigerator. I expected to someday expand my repertoire to include a giraffe. My parents did not buy me a penguin, they bought me cheap, dimestore turtles. I was known as "The Turtle Girl."

I later discovered an interest in tree climbing and became the neighborhood squirrel trainer. Quite proud of myself, I adorned my squirrels in doll clothes and the latest fashion accessories.

Years later, flipping through family photos, I noticed myself in a wide variety of cowgirl outfits with squirrels at my side. Had I always longed to be a cowgirl? I wore cowgirl outfits day in and day out, sometimes having to settle for simply a kerchief if my plastic cowgirl vest couldn't be found. I played baseball in a cowgirl outfit. I kissed my first boy in a cowgirl outfit. I attended Sunday School in a cowgirl outfit. I believe God understands cowgirls and forgives them their quirks.

Was the range my destiny? Every Sunday night I sat glued to the television set and longed to be a member of the Bonanza/Cartwright family. I empathized with each Cartwright dilemma and yearned to fly off the suburban carpet on my invisible horse. My friends thought my dad looked like Zorro, except my dad was an inner-city school teacher minus a mask and a sword. Instead of swords, he sometimes came up with a few switchblades confiscated from students. I took pride in the fact friends wanted to come to the Zorro House, and we kept our eyes open for anyone resembling Roy Rogers.

Roy Rogers was the coolest of dudes. Roy Rogers was the "King of the Cowboys." My father's name is Roy, and I also pretended to be related to the Rogers family. My parents honored me one birthday with a palomino plastic horse named, of course, Trigger.

It was my dream to someday ride a horse like Roy Rogers, get the bad guys, and watch truth prevail in the end. I still believe my plastic cowgirl outfit was fashioned after Roy's fancy fringes, and I sang all the Roy Roger's songs to anyone who would listen. We, the children of the earth, awarded Roy Rogers the Nobel Peace Prize, long ago.

Years later, the Midwestern Turtle Girl found herself heading up advertising campaigns for a major corporation. Callie Erickson fell in love with a good, tall, handsome Swede named Ludwig Oscar Carlson to coordinate with her Norwegian heritage.

Ludwig owned a small fleet of tractor-trailers, and was known as "The Salt Man." Ludwig also enjoyed pepper, however, his salt did not grace kitchen tables, it made roads negotiable in winter.

During their courtship, The Turtle Girl was swept off her feet when The Salt Man gave her a set of radial tires for Valentine's Day. Somewhat surprised, she exclaimed, "Wow! Thanks for the neat gift!" What impressed her most was that Ludwig cared about her safety. "I have to marry this man," she said. Ludwig is a salt-of-the-earth kind of guy.

Ludwig and Callie begat Little Baby PuLaRoo, better known as Kirsten in social circumstances and school. PuLaRoo grew up to be a fine, upstanding Third Grader. It was at that time our lives took an outrageous twist.

Instead of investing in real estate, Ludwig and I invested in pallets of books for PuLaRoo. Pu devoured each "horse" book in an hour. We could not keep the girl out of the saddle. Little did PuLaRoo know she was an original cowgirl wannabe. The broadening of our suburban horizons soon came to pass.

As I watched Pu play dolls with schoolmates, I wondered. Pu's fashion dolls housed their red and grey sports cars in tissue box garages. "Macy," Pu's favorite doll, flew off to Hawaii on business trips with my briefcase posing as an airplane. Macy soon had a maid, gold card, and a golf pro. Something had to change, and it wouldn't be the world around us. We needed to change. We began to make our way out of Plastic Land and into "What Have We Gotten Ourselves Into Land?" We decided to get back to nature.

Pu came up with an excellent suggestion. "Can I ride a real horse?" she begged and begged.

Getting out the trusty yellow pages, I located a riding stable. We knew nothing of life past suburban intersections. We drove for an hour and a half admiring the scenery and finally came to rest at Muddy Acres. Muddy Acres was in serious need of a hose, a broom, and a backhoe.

Muddy Acres featured a barn, fenced paddock, and a mentally deranged owner. Off to the side of the barn was a large kennel, complete with howling watch-dogs.

"Don't get too close," the owner/instructor warned us, "and whatever you do, don't stick your fingers in there."

Pu was thunderstruck. The wild-eyed instructor invited us into the barn while she muttered to herself and others we could not see. We peeked into each horse stall, and Pu observed, "Boy, that's a lot of poop."

We had to agree. From what Ludwig and I could see, each horse was standing on top of three feet of manure. The horses looked unnaturally tall.

"Yeah, I'm going to clean 'em out tomorrow," the equine authority informed us. "Now let's get you up on that horse," she winked broadly.

Pu mounted a horse and went through a visible transformation. She reminded me of the Madonna. I looked above Pu's head expecting to see a halo.

The instructor led Pu around on an Appaloosa for an hour, as the horse expertly sidestepped chunks of metal sticking out of the ground.

"I'll get that metal out tomorrow," she said with a far off look in her eyes. She then asked us into the house to sign an injury release form.

"Now, don't mind the pups. I'm trying to potty train them," she said, while attempting to open the backdoor. It took a couple of pushes, but there we were, trying to find our footing in the kitchen. If we thought the horses were having trouble balancing on three feet of manure, humans were having an even more difficult time maneuvering amongst dog doo-doo and soaked newspapers. This being our first time inside a human kennel, we minded our manners and refrained from choking.

Pups warmly greeted us, bowling us over. I made my way over to the single open chair. Six-foot-four Ludwig signed the injury release form, because I couldn't reach over the height of the table.

"I'm going to go through all this tomorrow," the instructor said, gesturing at the massively-high, piled paper-work on top of the table.

"Now, you're going to have to buy a riding hat," she announced, "Can't ride a horse without a riding hat!"

"You mean a cowboy hat?" I asked, eagerly. I envisioned all of us in cowboy hats. Changing our names to Cartwright, Ludwig and I could sport our cowboy hats on the driving range.

"No, protective head-gear. You need an official riding helmet."

The thought of falling off a horse had not occurred to me. I thought one simply stayed "on" the horse. Cartwrights do not fall off horses.

Pu's first homework assignment included locating a riding helmet. The nearest horse outfitter was actually located on our way back to the burbs, and if we hurried, it might still be open. We bid our new riding instructor farewell.

In the car, the three of us chatted excitedly about our adventure. Horse fever struck and we spiked perilous temperatures. Arriving at the equine supply store, Ludwig's mouth dropped open as though he were gazing upon the beginning of creation. In a fenced paddock south of the store, grazed the most magnificent animal.

Love at first bite, a grey Arabian nuzzled him. My husband changed before my startled eyes. The term "petting" took on new dimensions.

"Let's find out who owns this glorious animal," Ludwig shouted, gleefully.

He bounded into the store and drilled the occupants. Unaware of his new mission, I trailed behind. The riding hat suddenly took second place to the purchase of a horse.

"People buy horses all the time," Ludwig informed me, calmly.

I looked on in shock at this man I did not know. PuLaRoo danced across the store as though transported to heaven before her time.

"What do you mean people buy horses all the time?" I asked in astonishment. "We are not those people."

Ludwig attempted to explain why trucks and horses are similar. "Why do you think they call it horsepower?" he asked. The shopkeepers did not own the horse, but slipped Ludwig the telephone number of the person who did. Feeling frantic, I wondered if my husband would ever abandon this new Disney World. I finally managed to pull him out of the saddle display.

My cry was heard, and I was granted a miracle. Everybody got back into the car. Pu sat in the backseat, wearing her new riding helmet and looked decidedly dapper.

"Are you crazy?" I shouted in amazement.

"Uncle Dave wasn't crazy," Ludwig replied, with a far-off look in his eyes.

"What does Uncle Dave have to do with this?" I asked, trying to calm down. "Isn't he the uncle who sold you a used truck?"

Pu and I were treated to the brief history of Uncle Dave.

Now in his eighties, he broke broncos in his youth, and went on from horse-breaking to hauling agricultural commodities cross-country. "It was a natural transition," Ludwig insisted. Of course, this talent also coursed through his veins. "It runs in our family," Ludwig insisted of horse ownership. "Show me a trucker on the open road and I'll show you a cowboy. Riding highway is merely a substitute for riding fence."

Back home, I ran to the bathroom. I saw a man about a horse, while Ludwig inquired about one. I refused to come out.

"What's the animal's name?" was the most probing question Ludwig asked its owner.

Sitting in my study, recovering from the day's unexpectedness, the idea of owning a horse began to grow on me. I thought back to my beloved plastic cowgirl vest from years ago. Pu kept knocking on the door, shouting, "Does this mean we're going to get our own horse? Huh, Mom, huh?"

"We'll meet you there tomorrow at one o'clock," Ludwig instructed the receiver.

"Come on out, Mom!" Pu shouted, "Quick!"

The family excitement crescendoed and I faced the music. Pu hugged me and we bounced up and down in her delight.

"What's the horse's name?" I asked.

"Animal," replied Ludwig.

"I mean his name. I know he's an animal."

"Animal. His name is Animal," Ludwig insisted.

"Well, that's a funny name for a horse," I replied. Funny wouldn't be the half of it.

• • •

The next day all three of us saw one Ben Cutter, owner, about a horse and we ended up with one. Along with the purchase of our new pet came expenses. We turned into "boarders," which meant Animal could have his own downtown apartment for the price of his stall.

There is a lot to learn about ownership. For one thing, we thought we could ride the horse. "Oh, he isn't trained for that," answered Ben Cutter, our newest horse authority.

"What is he trained for?" we asked.

"You can lead him around in his halter and brush him," Ben replied. Seeing our dismay, he thought hard for a moment and added, "But I do have another horse for sale. It's Animal's sire."

"Is his father trained for brushing and walking?" we asked.

"Oh, no," he laughed, "he's trained for riding and driving."

"What does he drive?" I asked. "A mini-van?"

"Not exactly," Ben contemplated, "This horse won the Ohio Buckeye."

Ludwig laughed. "Now we're talking. Does he play football?"

"No, no, no. The Ohio Buckeye is a cart-driving event. This horse is famous, and he's sired some serious foals. He's very well trained."

Well trained, indeed. Our next visit caught him trying to mount the mare across the fence. Our neon sucker sign blinked, "Come and get us."

"Well, we really should get a horse we can ride," I offered. "It's silly to have one we can only look at."

We adopted Sam, a bay Arabian, into our family for a hefty price. We now owned two horses that needed brushing. We received a video tape of Sam winning the Buckeye. The video only cost us three thousand dollars.

Monthly expenses mounted. Something was seriously awry. It was ridiculous to pay someone to take care of our animals. Why not do it ourselves? Why not buy a farm? Buying a farm and putting the house up for sale seemed the obvious solution to our plight.

We spent weeks searching for real estate in a seventy mile radius of the city. Unable to locate the perfect nesting ground for our little brood, we desperately marched up to the door of an old farm house we'd admired from the road.

"Have you ever considered selling?" Ludwig asked the farmer, picturesque in tan, Carhartt bib overalls. He looked us up and down.

"Hmm . . . let me ask the Missus," he replied, slowly, wheels-a-turning.

He turned his head and she nodded, "Yes."

Recognizing the chance of a lifetime, the farmer chose early retirement.

"This farm has been in our family for three generations," he explained. "How soon do you want us out?"

Back home, in shock, sitting at our kitchen table, Ludwig and I poured over financial statements. "Do you think we can do it?" I asked, in terror.

"Sure, why not? It's not the end of the world. Have a little faith, Callie," Ludwig said, patting my shoulder. "If it doesn't work out, we can always come back to the city."

Only we didn't go back. We assumed the life of a pioneer in a modern world. I sold my corporate designer suits and bid adieu to one-hundred dollar salon appointments. We waved goodbye to the golf course and struck out on our own course.

Lord help us. We would need it.

Chapter Two

I'll Take the Lime Green House

Lester, our new contractor, scratched his head, rolled his eyes skyward, and winced. "I think the house has to come down."

Ludwig and I stood on the crumbling stoop and surveyed our lime-green farmhouse. "So what if the house is one-hundred years old? We can put in new carpet," Ludwig said, "Right, honey?"

We left Lester to figure it out. Lester is a short, wiry man in his fifties who, besides contracting, doubles as the mayor. Ludwig and I strolled down our gravel, half-a-mile long, country drive. We spotted red tractors in the distance, plowing up fields for spring planting. We were the proud owners of 140 acres of soybeans, corn, alfalfa, woods, two barns, chicken coop, corn crib, hog house and a one-hundred year old lime-green farmhouse. The air was crisp and the oxygen level high. We felt good, or maybe it was the unaccustomed oxygen less carbon monoxide.

We returned to the house to find Lester holding a sledge hammer. "We have to find out what's in back of these walls,' he told us, sternly.

"You mean punch a hole in the wall?" I asked, horrified.

"We have to see if you have any insulation. Sometimes these old farm houses don't have any. They used newspaper instead," the historian told us.

"Or maybe we have hidden treasure," I laughed. "Aren't old newspapers worth a lot of money?"

A two-foot-wide hole in the wall spoke reams of information. We did not have newspaper insulation, we had mouse dropping insulation. Mice ate the newspapers. From what we could tell, generations had come and gone. The new generation blinked back at us, offended at the intrusion.

"The electrical and plumbing are in really bad shape, too," Lester said, cheerfully. "We should take a look at the well, propane, and septic."

"Septic?" I asked. Totally ignorant, I believed one simply flipped a switch for the garbage disposal.

"We don't have sewage plants out here," Lester chuckled.

Good news did not greet us. Every inside wall of the house needed to come down. The electrical and plumbing had to be replaced.

"It's all downright dangerous," Lester informed us.

Our move into the new farm house was waylaid for months. PuLaRoo and I took up occupancy in a nearby deer-hunter's cabin, while Ludwig stayed in the city and drove out on weekends. One of us needed to oversee the operation, while the other sold the house in the city. We took bets on who would go insane first. I lost.

Although wired for electricity, the hunting cabin lacked heat and a telephone. Ludwig brought us a television, and in the evenings, Pu and I watched channel four. We did not need a television guide. Channel four was the only available channel. Pu and I had running water and a stove. What more could two girls want? Perhaps warm weather to continue.

Every morning the two of us supervised the farmhouse progress. As the days passed, I realized we required toilet facilities, so I rigged up my own septic system. "Porta-potty ala Callie" is quite simple. The workmen thought it ingenious. Two nylon straps taken from the middle of a lawn chair. One could take one's potty wherever one desired. I dug holes behind the silo and the barn. The only requirement: "Announce your destination."

"OK, who's got the potty?" became a common demand. "I'm going behind the silo," announced the most popular location because the views were so spectacular. You could see for thirty miles while sitting in your open study. Magazines and newspapers began turning up in the cornfield.

Fall approached, PMS possessed me. The cabin dropped to forty degrees at night. Pu and I fought over the portable electrical heater, stealing it from room to room. It wasn't hard to find, since there were only three rooms. Pu could hardly wait to get on the school bus in the morning because, "At least the school has heat!"

"That's it!" I shouted, pushed to the max. "We're going in!"

Lester and his three-man crew didn't know what had hit them. The soft-spoken woman from the far-off city gave a credible grizzly bear imitation.

"Do we have water?" I growled.

"Check," Lester answered startled.

"Do we have septic?"

"Check."

"Do we have heat?"

"Check."

"Then, you'll have to work around us. Get the suit-cases, Pu," said the bear to her cub.

"But the windows in the kitchen aren't in yet," Lester demurred.

"Frankly, Lester, I don't care!" I said throwing my arms up into the air.

All modesty flew out the window along with the fresh breezes through open kitchen windows.

"Morning, Lester, Al, Ron, Mike," I said, so sophisticated in my silk pajamas and robe. "You guys want eggs or cereal this morning?"

Accustomed to catered dinner parties, RSVPs, and ring before you come, I suddenly found myself living with four men, and my husband wasn't among them.

"I have to take a shower," I informed my harem, "will you get the phone?"

"Sure," Al said. "You want me to take messages?"

"Thanks, Al," I attempted a smile, "Can you catch the garbage?"

Sensing my slight impatience, Lester added, "We're almost done, Callie. I think you can call the movers."

All things come together for those who wait patiently.

I sang the Hallelujah chorus and called Ludwig.

"Great, I'll call the movers," he told me.

"You're not going to get those yahoos again, are you?" I asked diplomatically.

"They're professional movers, Callie, I know the guy who owns the company."

"You met him in a gin rummy game, Ludwig. He's

not working with a full deck."

I felt a chill setting in.

"I just don't want a repeat of our previous move," I continued, suddenly very wary. "I don't want to go through that nightmare again. Do you want me to come in and supervise?"

Ludwig was indignant. "I can handle this."

"And they'll pack everything? What about the glass-ware?"

"Callie," he insisted, "I'll handle it. They know what they're doing. Give it a rest."

A week later, I rested uneasily. I glanced at my watch. I trusted Ludwig's good intentions, but I sure didn't trust the movers. I raised the sweats just thinking about it.

I suspected the moving company didn't even have salaried employees. They plucked transients off the rail-road tracks and gave them a job for the day. I could just see them holding up a sign, RIP-OFF CALLIE DAY. If you want to get paid and steal her blind, get on the bus."

Hours into the waiting, I called Ludwig. He answered sheepishly, "We're running a little late. The movers didn't show up with packers."

Unsurprised, I asked, "So, how long is it going to take?"

"I'm not sure," he hesitated, "I called some people."

"People? What people? What's going on there, Ludwig?" I asked, suspiciously.

"Well, the movers said they don't do packing. They're having breakfast right now. Egg and cheese sandwiches."

"What 'people' did you call?" I prodded.

I heard Ludwig whispering into a crackling short-wave radio in the background.

"What do you mean, 'When can who get there,' Ludwig?" I asked.

Ludwig didn't answer. My worst nightmare came true. Ludwig was packing glassware.

"Why don't I get in the car right now?" I asked.

"We can handle it. No need to worry. We'll be out there this afternoon, it's going really fast."

How fast can packing glassware go? Apparently, pretty fast when you just throw them in a box. I waited on pins and needles while supervising the last of the painting in the kitchen. Cracking my whip, I told Harry, the painter, that he and his crew needed to be out in two hours.

"No, problem, Callie," Harry replied, cheerfully.

"How are you coming with the carpet-laying, Lester?" I yelled.

"Pretty soon, Callie, pretty soon." He was confidence itself.

Pu skipped school that day to help with the move and was about to be a witness to her mother's nervous breakdown. A caravan of semi tractor-trailers and a moving van appeared in the driveway. Men and women I had never laid eyes on jumped out of their cabs.

I was right. Ludwig had put out a CB alert. These are the kind strangers who had packed my underwear. Truckers are always glad to lend a hand.

"Where do you want us to put the intimate apparel?" asked a man of tall stature.

"Up in the intimate section of the house," I replied, "Bedroom is to the right."

The male truckers supervised my underwear drawers, and the female truckers, the kitchen dishes. The yahoos manhandled the furniture.

"See?" said Ludwig, cheerfully. "I told you we would make it. And you were worried."

For three hours chaos whirled around me.

Overwhelmed, I stood in the kitchen doorway as the man of tall stature, winked at me. Harry accidentally spilled a gallon of white paint on the kitchen floor. A woman putting away dishes slipped on the paint and screamed, "End-Dump" before she hit the floor. Two pneumatic semi-drivers hoisted her to her feet.

Ludwig's gin rummy hustler announced, "There's a man who wants to see you."

I glanced out into the yard and spotted a man holding a clipboard. He waved to me and yelled, "Building Inspector!"

I looked at Lester who vanished into the next room.

"Can I see your permit?" the building inspector asked.

"What permit?" I asked, truly innocent of all charges.

Before the inspector answered, Lester, Al, Ron, and Mike filed past me, tools in hand.

"Where are you going?" I asked Lester in bewilderment. "You're not finished!"

"Oh, yes we are," replied Lester. "We're out of here."

Unaware I was in incipient cardiac arrest, Ludwig asked, "What are you serving for lunch? And where's the beer? The movers want their beer."

Not being one to faint, I exploded. Or imploded, as the case may be. People dropped what they were doing to watch the show.

"The woman's gone mad," the men whispered.

I put my hands over my ears so I wouldn't hear myself scream. "I CAN'T TAKE ANYMORE! THIS IS IT, THIS IS MY BREAKING POINT! EVERYBODY OUT!"

"But we have to finish the second coat of paint," Harry tried sweet reason.

"FORGET THE PAINT!" I screamed. "EVERYBODY OUT! I WANT MY HOUSE BACK!"

The women tried to reason with me. "Callie, you can't get your house back, if you don't let us finish," they said in sweet, reasonable tones.

The women knew. They knew all about the pressures of a move. They understood percolating hormones. They recognized an obsessive nesting syndrome when they saw one.

Everybody cleared out. The men stood on one side of the lawn, the women on the other. I started to weep uncontrollably. "Let her have a good cry," the women said, patting my shoulder.

"You don't know what it's been like," I said to my surrogate therapists. "And strange men are walking around with my underwear," I sobbed.

"It will be okay, dear," they reassured me. "We're almost done."

"Do you think so?" I asked through my tears. "Done?" I replied, whispering the unattainable word.

"Yes, done," replied my guardian angels.

With their arms around me, the angels helped me over to the men who were wide-eyed at this female display.

"She's all right, now," the head therapist told the men.

"Break's over!" yelled the gin hustler. "Back to work!" The building inspector left in a huff and promised to return. Little did I know Lester hightailed it to the county courthouse in his red pickup truck. Using his mayoral influence, he filed a permit even before the ambitious inspector reached his desk.

All things work together for good.

The transient movers walked off with little things we only noticed missing six months later. I imagined PuLaRoo's stylish watches gracing many a wrist down by the railroad tracks. Ludwig bought out the hardware store, because all of his prized tools had disappeared. He doggedly refused to admit any theft occurred, and is, five years later, still searching for his beloved, gas-operated weed whip.

Traveling to the grocery store, I noticed neatly trimmed edges along the railroad tracks. I waved to a man holding a gas-operated weed whip. I pulled over and asked him the time. Sporting a fashion doll-faced watch, he told me it was time to "mind my own business."

Farm business did, indeed, await.

Chapter Three

Chicken Stew

A good Girl Scout is always prepared. Absent on the day they taught survival, I operate on a wing and a prayer. I bought knee pads.

Even before our move to the farm, I researched horses, hogs, and poultry. My desk in the city was strewn with books and pamphlets from all across America on the husbandry of these animals. I did not request all this lore, Ludwig unilaterally decided I required a new career, once we landed. I am the family librarian and try to retain all knowledge and papers till death do us part.

Raising a few chickens came to mind. I reread the pamphlet titled, "The Small Poultry Flock," and anxiety set in at the thought of actually going ahead with my scheme. I did not inform Ludwig or PuLaRoo. What if I chickened out?

I reread the small ad in the local paper, "Bantam chickens and a peacock."

I called my new friend, Millie. Millie lives down the road a spell. I asked Millie if she wanted to go chicken shopping and look at a peacock.

"You mean go to the grocery store and the zoo?" she asked.

I elaborated. "No. I need help, Millie! What if I get lost on those country roads? What am I going to do with the chickens, once I get them in the truck?"

"Well, I'm not sure what I can do," she replied chuckling, "but sure, I'll come with you."

I hopped into my new-used, brown pickup truck that Ludwig had presented to me just two days before. "You need a truck if you live on a farm," he said. PuLaRoo had ooed and awed over the fact her mother would become a truck driver. "You'll get used to the wide turns," Ludwig informed me.

This was all well and fine, but I felt like I was driving a boat down the highway. I pulled up in front of Millie's house, struggling to turn the wheel because I was stuck in four-wheel drive. "Life preservers are in the back," I told Millie.

A tiny woman in her sixties, Millie once had designs on joining the Canadian Mounties. Millie may be missing the uniform, but the attitude remains. Rural life suits her because she can target shoot in her back yard. We don't need an alarm clock, because Millie starts her practice at seven a.m.

A line from the chicken pamphlet crept into my thoughts. "Cannibalism among chickens is always a distinct possibility." I envisioned scenes from Alfred Hitchcock's, "The Birds." I hoped the chickens had eaten breakfast.

Millie and I thought we were lost. Millie sympathized with my fear of taking a wrong turn and getting fatally confused in a cornfield forever. We weren't really lost, though, and we soon arrived at our destination; a scene right out of the movie "Deliverance." The owner of the property was apparently operating his own private landfill. The only thing missing was the banjo player.

"They'll never find us out here," I whispered to Millie.

Millie was unshaken. "This is the country, Callie! This is normal. Come on, let's go get your chickens," she laughed.

A man wearing tan, Carhartt bib overalls came out of the house and motioned for us to follow him. He led us to a small shed out back. I felt like I was walking to my execution. Did chickens actually exist on this farm? Sudden enthusiastic squawking reassured me.

The man, minus most of his teeth grinned, opened the shed door, and whistled, "He lost his feathers during a fox fight. His tail will grow back," he pointed at the peacock. "His name is Stanley. How many do you want?" he asked.

"I'll take all of them," I volunteered, hoping to get out of the situation alive. My former negotiating skills went out the window, "How much do you want for them? Do you take credit cards?"

"Cash," Millie said turning to me. "You have to pay cash. It's not reported income, is it?" she conspiratorially winked at the toothless man.

I decided not to get on my high-horse about income tax. I was willing to sign over the title papers to the pickup, if it would ensure our safe departure.

"But you have to give us that chicken-catcher," Millie insisted. A chicken catcher is a long wire with a hook on the end that looks like a coat hanger.

The man agreed to the terms and stuffed the birds into gunny sacks. My legs wobbled, as I walked to the pickup.

"It was nice meeting you," I smiled. Politeness over terror.

The man smiled back. Obviously, preventive dental care was not a priority. I made a mental note to check for gingivitis upon returning home.

"Isn't this fun?" I asked through clenched teeth, while Millie and I drove the back roads with a peacock and ten chickens in the backseat. Bouncing in and out of gravel ruts, I developed instant shoulder tendonitis and almost broke the steering wheel with my grip.

Millie, that tough old bird, and I looked at each other with fear in our eyes. Stanley, the tawdry-tailed peacock instigated a jailbreak. The confederate chickens burst into a chorus of, "We're coming to get you." Eleven beaks poked through gunny sacks. I recited the Lord's Prayer.

Risking life and limb, Millie gallantly offered to sit in the backseat with the rebel chickens. Also a gourmet cook, she hissed, "Stop or you're pate!" which only made matters worse.

The chickens did not take well to ultimata and we quickly changed our tune, cooing to the chickens as if they were our children, "It's all right, we're almost home now." Miraculously, it worked.

Arriving at the barn with sighs of relief, we pulled the gunny sacks out, as though we were handling poisonous snakes. We untied the bags, looked down, and waited. Nothing happened.

"Do you think they're dead?" I asked Millie, quickly assessing possible burial sites on the farm, wondering if I could beat Ludwig's and Pu's arrival and hide the evidence.

Trying to pump up my courage, I announced, "Well,

somebody's got to get them out of there." Dumping the chickens onto the ground, I poked them with the chicken catcher. Before you could say "chicken stew," they jumped and flew all over the barn.

"I didn't kill them!" I shouted with glee. "They were just sleeping!"

Ludwig and Pu returned home and delighted in my new purchase. We all looked forward to fresh eggs by the morning. However, the poultry saga was far from over. Two chickens disappeared overnight, and the insides of the barn walls came alive with sounds of music. Chickens squawked back and forth to each other, as we discovered the two missing ones caught between the barn wall and horse-stall wall. The stall walls are over ten-feet high and there is a foot of space between the two.

Ludwig hoisted me up, and I put a flashlight down the foot-wide crack. "They're in there all right," I said regarding a pair of beaks. This was to be our first out of many animal rescue missions.

"Let's get them out tomorrow," Ludwig said in best Scarlett fashion. "I have to get to work. The county is calling for salt."

"We can't just leave them in there," I contended.

Ludwig responded by dumping a glob of recently-fallen snow on top of their heads, and pelted them with corn kernels from above. The chickens clucked back, thankfully, while Ludwig left for work.

Upon Ludwig's return from America's workforce, we resumed our mission. We came up with a plan. In typical farm-fashion, we armed ourselves with duct tape.

We duct-taped the chicken catcher to a broom handle. We placed a ladder against the stall wall. However, the stall wall is slanted, following the curve of the Quonset building, so I held on for dear life while trying gamely to balance, hold a flashlight and chicken-catcher-broom, all at once.

Ludwig said, "Let me take first crack at it," and I gladly forked over my position.

"This is just like playing 'Go Fish' at a carnival!" Ludwig's early enthusiasm was contagious.

Hours went by and he no longer found it amusing. Ten feet below he had to snag a chicken leg, turn the animal upside down, and then pull it up by its feet. Ludwig finally snagged a foot, and as the chicken made its way upward, Ludwig accidentally dropped the flashlight. The chicken spiraled downward and sat on the flashlight. We were in the dark.

"Have any more flashlights?" Ludwig asked, hopefully.

I ran to the house and quickly analyzed my "There-Might-Be-A-Nuclear-War-Someday" supplies in the cellar. Two flashlights, four cans of beans and three rolls of toilet paper. I noted that we would last about a week, and I grabbed a flashlight.

We resumed the rescue. Finally, after too many hours of standing on the ladder, Ludwig whispered, "I've got one."

As Ludwig lofted the chicken skyward, we cheered. One down, one to go. It was my turn. Active duty was presented to me as though I were headed for Omaha Beach. Ludwig carefully went over the instructions, informing me on the dos and don'ts of a hostage rescue.

I saluted and took my position on the ladder of soon-to-be success. I wielded the chicken catcher broom with the skill of a neurosurgeon. My only mistake was talking once I'd snagged a leg.

I had the chicken upside down and began celebrating. Squawk, squawk, squawk, drop. It took another hour before I was advised to "keep your mouth shut this time."

I told myself not to breathe. Sighs of relief were heard throughout the barn. "We got her!" we shouted. The chicken acted as though our efforts were inconsequential.

Utterly exhausted, I asked, "What time is it?"

Hours upon hours had passed.

"Boy, am I hungry," announced Ludwig. "What's for dinner?"

I looked at Ludwig in astonishment that he could even ask the question. "Chicken. Chicken is for dinner."

• • •

"Hey, Ludwig, come here!" I shouted. "Bring PuLaRoo!"

Easter arrived months early for the Carlsons. Ludwig and Pu ran out of the house thinking I was in the midst of an emergency. "Look!" I exclaimed.

Lo and behold, little brown eggs from the Bantam hens lay scattered amongst hay bales. My decorative chickens actually sprouted eggs. We laughed in amazement. All three of us joined in the egg hunt, running here and there shouting, "Here's another one!"

As we gathered up the eggs, I had tears in my eyes. I thought of manna--the heavenly food God provided the Israelites in the desert. My manna took the form of little brown eggs. I reveled in the moment of heavenly wonder, observing in Biblical '90s fashion, "This is so cool."

"Can we eat these?" Pu asked, interrupting my heavenly reverie.

"Of course, Pu," I replied. "We can eat these, right, Ludwig?" I asked my egg expert.

"Fresh off the farm, Callie," Ludwig answered. "Where do you think grocery stores get theirs?" he laughed.

We hurried into the house with our manna. While I heated a frying pan, Pu cracked the eggs.

"What's wrong with these eggs, Mom?" she asked. Pu took a step back from the bowl like something was going to bite her.

"Hmm," I said looking over her shoulder. "They are a little dark, aren't they? And they're so . . . perky."

"Perky eggs?" asked Ludwig. "How can an egg look perky?"

Ludwig came over to see for himself. "Oh, that's just because they're fresh," he chuckled. "The yolk stands up higher when they're fresh. You're just used to eggs that have been sitting around for weeks at the grocery store."

"But why are the yolks so dark, Ludwig?" I asked.

"They're dark because they don't come from a white hen. You've got Bantam chickens," declared the poultry expert.

Pu's eyes grew big as yolks and she informed us, "You're not going to make me eat those dark, perky eggs."

"Then your father and I will enjoy the dark, perky eggs," I announced, as only a mother could. "You don't know what you're missing."

Ludwig and I sat down to our breakfast of over-easy eggs.

Pu looked on with interest. Dark, perky yolks stared back at me.

"Poke, 'em, Mom," Pu suggested.

"You don't think there's a baby chicken in there, do you, Ludwig?" I asked.

"Doesn't matter, Callie. Doesn't matter if it's fertilized, because it's too fresh," he said wolfing his eggs.

Pu looked at me with her I-told-you-so face. I defied her, and poked my eggs. I swabbed them with toast and munched slowly. I couldn't swallow. My stomach resisted dark, perky eggs.

"How about if I buy some white chickens?" I asked the group.

"These are good . . . really," Ludwig said, ever the supportive husband.

"Then why haven't you cleaned your plate?" I asked.

Ludwig hesitated, caught in the act. "Well," he admitted, "they are a little on the perky side."

Pu's eyes widened and she gave me her "See?" expression.

I expected a lightning bolt from heaven. We wouldn't make very good Israelites, wandering in the desert. The Israelites would have welcomed dark, perky eggs.

• • •

Later that morning I went on a hunt for white chickens. White chickens = white eggs. No problem.

Not hard to find chickens in a farming community. All I had to do was look in the local paper. Bounty abounds. I already owned gunny sacks. I flew solo on the white chicken purchase.

Arriving at my destination, I confronted chicken heaven. "How many do you want?" asked the man wearing tan, Carhartt bib overalls.

"Oh, maybe ten," I replied.

"The birds are out back," he said. "Give you a real good deal on all of them."

He opened the chicken coop door and I experienced an assault on my allergies. Five hundred chickens did not sit well with my nose. Blinded by watery eyes, I asthmatically picked my birds. I picked the big ones. Bigger is better. Big chickens mean "extra large" eggs.

We could have used my handy-dandy chicken catcher. Feathers flew everywhere, and distinguishing one chicken from the next was impossible. I wondered if I would die of suffocation. Ludwig and Pu did not know my whereabouts. The headlines would read, "Allergy Sufferers Beware."

• • •

Meanwhile, back at the farm, my new white chickens woke up the moment I dumped them on the ground. Days went by as we waited for our farm fresh eggs.

Each morning I checked the chicken coop only to find one egg. We started fighting over who ate the farm fresh egg, and the chickens started fighting over who would kill each other first. I looked on in shock, thinking, "Cannibalism."

The smallest chicken of the bunch, Little Mel, started losing her hair, or rather, her feathers. The larger chickens gathered round her and picked on her, literally. Every time one of us left the house we yelled, "Quit pickin' on Little Mel!"

I expected the Chicken Humane Society to show up any second. Little Mel went completely bald and was not getting along well with others. When Harvey the plumber came to the house, he noticed bald Little Mel running in circles out in the driveway. "I just don't know what's wrong, Harvey," I told him. "They keep picking on her."

Harvey chortled. "That's because they're all roosters, Callie! Except that one," he said pointing to Little Mel.

"But they're all white!" I exclaimed. "White chickens are supposed to be female!"

"Not if they're roosters!" yelled Harvey practically bursting his pipes.

We transferred Little Mel to a new dormitory on campus. The Bantam chickens welcomed her with open wings. Little Mel kept her end of the bargain and continued to produce her daily, farm fresh egg.

Encouraged by our egg production, we expanded our animal kingdom.

Chapter Four

Hog Heaven

Every farm requires a pet pig. "Let me just run up to Leroy's and buy one of those cute little pink pigs," I told Ludwig and Pu.

Leroy is the local hog producer wide open to parting with one of his babies for forty dollars.

"Oh, no," Ludwig and Pu replied. "We want one of those pigs from California."

Pot-bellied pigs were not overrunning the nation at that point in time. They were hybrid, mail-ordered, and quite expensive. Pu and Ludwig researched national pot-bellied pig articles and many dollars in phone calls later, we had a match. The "Pig People" approved us as an adoptive family.

Some people just know how to fly, and little Elmer was no exception.

Elmer chalked up 2,000 miles on Northwest Airlines, arriving in a crate with his Baba blanket and Santa Claus squeeze toy. The accompanying note from the breeder said, "Elmer is potty trained and he enjoys a good swim in the pool." Most Midwest farms do not have a swimming pool in the backyard. Adopted into newly-poor, farm family, Elmer would have to sacrifice and do his laps in the bathtub.

Weighing in at twenty-six pounds, Elmer struggled pigfully as Ludwig and Pu hoisted him up over the rim of the tub. I gladly forked over my childhood dream of owning a penguin. I couldn't exactly keep Elmer in the freezer, but he sure could swim in my bathtub.

Elmer did not like the bathtub. Elmer did not like bath water, period. Elmer's squeals may have closed the Black Hole. I had no idea such surround sound was available in our universe.

Elmer's squeals eclipsed our own.

"Get Elmer out of the tub!" I yelled.

Retrieving a slippery, wet, twenty-six-pound pig from the bathtub is not an easy task. Ludwig crawled into the bathtub with Elmer. Elmer attempted to escape Ludwig's clutches by flinging himself against the enamel walls of the tub.

Continuing to squeal at the top of his lungs, Elmer flailed wildly, certain he was headed for the barbeque spit.

"Don't let him drown!" Pu and I cried.

I flailed wildly trying to locate towels to dam up the bathroom doorway. A small lake formed, flooding the dining room. It is not every house whose bathroom adjoins the dining room. Pu stood in terror, covering her ears.

Ludwig attempted to roll Elmer over the edge of the tub, creating tsunami waves. A woman's thoughts can be serendipitous. I thought of real estate disclosures. "To your knowledge, have you ever had water damage?" the form would ask. I would be honor-bound to check, "Yes."

I took the path of least resistance. I joined the circus and climbed into the tub with Elmer and Ludwig. Ludwig took Elmer's front end, I took the back. How Ludwig and I won the slippery pig contest, I do not know. Elmer plopped over the edge and righted himself.

He shook himself off and snorted at us.

"Mom, Elmer needs his baby oil," Pu remembered. In their travels through magazine articles on pot-bellied pigs, Pu and Ludwig had learned that Elmer is prone to dry skin. Pot-bellied pigs must be kept lubricated at all times.

"Who would like to do the honors?" I asked.

Little did we know what a torturous project lay ahead. Pu squirted a heavy stream of baby oil onto Elmer's back. Elmer resisted lubrication. Elmer squealed, ran out of the bathroom, into the dining room, ran laps around the table, and played hide-and-seek between the table legs. He glared at us like a bull ready to charge. Pu took a run at Elmer and squirted baby oil into the air. One lubricated chandelier.

I threw up my arms in disbelief. "Forget the baby oil," I told Pu, "Elmer will learn to live with dry skin."

"Should I get his Baba, Mom?" Pu asked.

Elmer snatched his Baba from Pu, found Santa Claus, and waltzed over to the expensive living room couch. He blinked back at us, innocently.

"What does he want?" we wondered.

Done with his Saturday night bath, Elmer was ready for bed. "I think he wants a lift," said Ludwig.

"I'm not going to have a pig on my expensive couch!" I replied, pointing to the couch.

Elmer launched a life-threatening, heart-attack, inducing squeal.

"All right, already! Put Elmer up on the couch!" I

surrendered.

Elmer settled into his new home cuddled in his Baba blanket. He slept like a baby with his head resting on a white down pillow. Morning came and we wondered if the first half of Elmer's instructions held spoken truth. Was Elmer potty trained?

Elmer was potty trained. He slid off the well-oiled couch, and flew out the front door like a shot out of a cannon. We watched Elmer sniff around the front yard. Satisfied he could be left alone for a few minutes, we retreated inside for breakfast.

After finishing his farm fresh egg, Ludwig opened the front door. "Ah . . . Callie . . . you'd better come have a look. You know those seeds you ordered for next spring? You can plant them now."

Within fifteen minutes flat, Elmer had dug us a twelve-foot-by-five-foot garden. Never mind that its locale was the middle of the front lawn. Elmer's instructions had failed to mention he came with his own plow.

"I think you can cancel the rental on the Merry Tiller," said Ludwig.

Elmer glanced up from his work and snorted through his mud-covered snout. Satisfied with his plowing, he wanted back into the house. He refused to wipe his feet.

"Ah, come on, Mom, let Elmer back into the house," Pu pleaded.

"This is a farm house," Ludwig reminded me.

"Does that mean we have to live like pigs?" I couldn't resist.

Elmer snorted back at me, whizzed past, and flung

open the door with his snout.

"Are you coming?" Elmer seemed to ask. He toddled into the kitchen, went straight to his feeding dish, and looked up at me, expectantly.

"I think he wants breakfast," Ludwig said.

I looked into the refrigerator. "What would make Elmer happy?"

The "other white meat" stared back at me.

"Elmer, dear, would you like some bacon?"

• • •

Elmer made himself totally at home, coming and going as he pleased. He managed to make a few friends, first among them, Sparky the dog, a Border Collie cross.

Sparky is our flea market dog. A flea market is a huge garage sale minus the garages. We wandered by a little girl sitting on a bench holding up a sign "free dog." Not ones to bypass anything free, the Carlsons took Sparky home.

A free wonder-dog, Sparky's feats include climbing twenty-foot ladders and saving small children from potential disasters. Not to be outdone by a measly pig, Sparky took her alpha role dead seriously. Sparky became Elmer's Entertainment Director.

One day, Elmer was hard at work lounging under his favorite tree. Glancing out the window, I noticed Sparky carrying an ice cream bucket by the handle.

"What in the world?" I thought.

Sparky trotted the ice cream bucket over to Elmer, who perked up at the possibility of food.

"Ludwig and Pu, you have to come and see this," I called.

"Where did she get the ice cream bucket?" Ludwig asked.

"I have no idea, but look, she's taking something white out of the bucket."

"I think it's a baseball," Pu said.

"Wherever in the world did she get a baseball?" I asked.

Sparky lay three feet away from Elmer and rolled the ball to him. Elmer obliged and returned the ball. Back and forth, back and forth went the game.

Wondering if they required extra players, the three of us hurried out to join them. Clutching the portable phone, I tried to get the "World of Baseball" on the line. It would be a first.

A ten million-dollar contract was not in our future.

Instead of a baseball, Ludwig's farm fresh egg rolled between our legs. When it came to playing egg-toss with Elmer, Sparky made her own rules. Spoons were out and snouts were in.

We scrambled for the egg, and Elmer rolled on top of it over-easy. Our hopes poached, we tried to look at the sunny-side.

Almost to the boiling point, Ludwig said, "That fries it."

"But remember, Ludwig," I told him, "we have to crack a few eggs to make an omelette."

• • •

Every farm requires two pet pigs. We believed in the Noah theory. Every animal deserves a pal. I agreed to let Elmer purchase a sibling.

It only took a short time for some local farmers to figure out that pot-bellied pigs are, indeed, pigs in a poke. Already having the breeding facilities available, they began to flood the market with pot-bellied pigs. Launching pot-bellied pigs in record numbers, swine farmers squealed all the way to the bank.

On our countryside rambles, our old game of finding letters in the alphabet on road signs, turned to pig-spottings. Pu is the natural leader, due to the fact that she takes the school bus each morning, while mother is stuck at home feeding animals and father keeps his eyes on the road while driving seventy miles to work.

Our next addition did not arrive from a California breeder via Northwest Airlines. It came from a mother with five kids in the backseat of a van at a gas station. Hearing squeals from the pump next to us, we peered inside the van. Yes sir, we had us a pig-spotting.

The little black pig was no bigger than a pound of bacon. Not one to play shy, Ludwig struck up a conversation with our pump neighbor, quickly outlining our life history to the harried mother while she pumped gas. I lunged for the door handle when Ludwig began explaining PuLaRoo's delivery.

"Yes, well it's very nice to meet you, too," I told the mother.

"She lives over by the cement plant," Ludwig offered.

"Oh, how nice," I replied, knowing he just might invite them all to dinner. "We know the cement plant well.

We bought a new foundation from them."

"Do you have a lot of those cute little pigs?" Ludwig asked. The woman looked to the interior of her van and watched as the children planted the pig's face against a window. They made pig nose prints on the windows to match their own.

"This little piggy is going to market," the mother replied. "I'll sell him to you for a tank of gas."

We could not believe our good fortune. Pu cuddled the piglet in her arms, as we waved goodbye to our new friends.

Meanwhile, back at the farm, Elmer slept peacefully under his oak tree, awaking to little piglet snorting sounds. Absolutely overjoyed, he ran over to us as fast as his short legs could carry him. No longer the twenty-six-pound pig, Elmer now transported his fifty pounds adroitly.

"What did you bring me?" he cried through his snout.

A wild snorting session erupted. The piglet wanted down and Elmer wanted up. "Okay, let's put him down and see what happens," I suggested.

Little snout met big snout, and we believe Elmer shed tears. They scurried across the lawn dashing to and fro. Happiness soon overwhelmed Elmer, and it was time for another nap. Settling down, the tiny piglet tried to roll Elmer over on his side. Elmer was bemused, but decided to oblige his new friend.

"What should we name him, Pu?" I asked.

"Wilbur, Mom, his name is Wilbur."

"Of course. Of course, his name is Wilbur," I said.

We regarded our new Wilbur in disbelief. Rolled

over, Elmer lay in shock, as Wilbur attempted to nurse from him.

"He thinks Elmer is his mother!" I exclaimed.

Elmer eyeballed us back, wanting to know what was going on.

Even though Elmer is male, he still has rows of nipples. Wilbur wanted one.

"This is so cute!" exclaimed Pu.

Elmer disagreed violently and attempted to escape. Wilbur trailed him across the farm. Elmer finally gave up and plopped over on his side. One happy piglet, Wilbur nursed from his new mother.

"Elmer's getting in touch with his feminine side," I told Pu.

"Is the feminine side the right side or the left side, Mom?" Pu asked.

"Probably the left side," I chuckled, grinning at Ludwig.

• • •

Like it or not, certain services need to be performed on farm animals. Wilbur required neutering which, in farm terms, is a gentle way of saying castration. Un-neutered pigs can be a handful and lean toward aggression.

Assured by my new best friend, the vet, I brought Wilbur to his office for elective surgery. I carried Wilbur into the waiting room and sat, surrounded by cat and dog owners. I held a pig on my lap, nodding to all the amused stares.

"Callie, you can bring him in now," the vet's assistant

told me.

A hard cold table awaited Wilbur. Sensing my sudden uncertainty, the assistant told me, "This will only take a minute."

She glanced at me sideways, wondering if I was going to pass out. "Why don't you wait outside?" she asked. "I mean, way outside. Why don't you wait in your truck? Put some nice music on the radio, it will make you feel better."

Good idea, I thought. I walked past four people holding dogs and cats. They smiled at me, knowingly.

In the truck, I took a deep breath. Tuning the radio, I cranked up the volume full blast. Ah, some nice classical music. Pamela Ross at the piano.

But wait, who goes there? Through the window of the building, I saw frenzy. People dashed from one end of the waiting room to the other. Arms up in the air, leashes flying, dog meeting cat, horror-struck faces. I rolled down the window to investigate.

With the window open, I could hear squeals radiating from the building. Pet owners leapt frenziedly, clasping their hands over their ears. The ones still sitting in chairs rocked back and forth, desperately trying to hang onto their animals.

One brave soul shouldered the door open. Shooting me an angered, horrified, bullet of a look, he fled into a nearby soybean field with his cocker spaniel in tow. Wilbur's squeals followed him.

Jammed in the doorway, others tried to follow. Putting their differences aside, dogs and cats fled in unison. Only one small boy with a dog in his arms remained in the building. Wilbur's squeals continued, as the little boy rocked from side to side in his chair, helpless to free himself from the mayhem. Caught in a tangled leash, his beloved retriever thrust himself in the air and catapulted back from the force. I untangled the leash, scooped up the boy, and headed for the door. The retriever flew past us, the vet's assistant following on his heels.

"We're done now," she said. "You can take Wilbur home."

"Do I want to take Wilbur home?" was my question.

She giggled. "He's fine! Dr. Nabours will give you instructions."

Dr. Nabours came into the waiting room holding a bewildered Wilbur. "Now, you have to keep him quiet for three days," he said, while massaging his ear drums.

"Keep Wilbur quiet?" I asked.

"Here's your pig," he said as he placed Wilbur in my arms.

Keep Wilbur quiet? When pigs fly . . .

Chapter Five

Hook, Line, and Sinker

Bundling my baby home from the hospital, I reviewed the medical instructions in my mind, while trying to keep my eyes on the road. "Keep him in a dark, quiet room for three days. Separate him from other pigs. Bring Wilbur back in ten days for suture removal."

Ludwig and Pu met me in the driveway, two pictures of concern. "How did it go?"

"I think we've been blacklisted from the community," I responded. When I relayed the surgical shenanigans, Ludwig and Pu agreed that Mother was now in charge of all veterinary services.

"I hope you know, I'll hear about this at school," Pu said.

"Well, let's just get him settled," I sighed.

Plopping Wilbur down in the guest bedroom and drawing the curtains was not an option. Wilbur would expect a breakfast tray and a rose. We put the convalescent in a small pole building, laid him on blankets, and brought him homemade chicken-noodle soup.

The square pole building is an extra garage of sorts, housing everything from alfalfa seeds to fishing gear. Not equipped with an overhead door, it has a sliding door with a heavy latch to hold it tight from blizzard breezes.

Getting on our hands and knees, we toddler-proofed the building. Or so we thought. Satisfied it was secure and pig-proof, we walked back into the house. Wilbur, full of chicken-noodle soup, slept soundly.

I let Elmer out the backdoor for his afternoon rendevous with nature. It took him two seconds to grow suspicious. As I looked out the dining room window, Elmer had his nose to the ground, with his friend, Sparky, hard on his heels. The two turned a one-eighty and made a beeline for the pole building. Using his snout, Elmer discovered a half-inch crack at the door connection of the pole building. He and Sparky busily sniffed the crack, snorting and whining. Squeals suddenly erupted from inside the building. I raced out the door shouting, "Wilbur, you're supposed to keep quiet for three days!"

I opened the service door to the building, snapped on the light, and almost passed out from the volume. A metal building amplifies sound. Wilbur's screams ricocheted off the metal sides, practically rupturing my eardrums.

Stunned by the sheer intensity, focusing was impossible. Wilbur stood in the center of the floor, hyperventilating and wailed. The large sliding door began to crash against its doorframe. Attempting to tear the two-hundred-pound door out of its sliding-track, Elmer's snout thrust through the crack. The Jaws of Life had new meaning.

Truly alarmed, I saw that Wilbur had something sticking out of his mouth. It looked like a worm. A worm with a nylon line attached to it. Dashing about, I located a fishing pole now lying on the cement floor. Wilbur was attached to the end of the line. The hook was stuck firmly in his mouth.

I slid out the service door and yelled, "Somebody help!" to anyone listening. "Somebody" was Elmer and Sparky who seemed to understand the word "help" immediately.

"Mom's in trouble!" is what they understood. "Let's crack this puppy open!"

I don't know how they did it, but they snapped a two-hundred pound door off its track. Not only that, they ripped a blizzard-proof door latch off the frame.

The door crashed onto the driveway barely missing my head. Wilbur stood in the center of the shambles for about three seconds. Let Freedom Ring!

Wilbur departed the building, the fishing pole bouncing behind him. Very proud of their successful mission impossible, Elmer and Sparky took flight on the heels of the freed inmate. This encouraged Wilbur to increase his speed.

Running as fast as I could, I threw myself on top of the fishing pole as it whizzed past. This, of course, created another dilemma, because Wilbur was still attached to the other end. Forced to keep up with Wilbur, I traveled two laps around the house until he got tired. Ludwig and Pu finally looked up from watching TV to see me periodically flying past the living-room window.

By the time they reached the door and stood on the back stoop, Wilbur had stopped for a breather. I held a rod and reel in my hand, with a pig as my fresh catch of the day.

"Let me tell you about the one that got away," I huffed.

"Oh, my word!" exclaimed Ludwig, "Did he swallow the hook?"

"He took the bait. The hook is stuck in his tongue. He tried to eat the little piece of worm left on the hook." Wilbur gathered himself, ready to sprint again. "Quick, run and get the ginger snap cookies!" I cried.

Bribing him with his favorite snack, we were able to make Wilbur sit still long enough for us to remove the fishing hook. Ludwig wrestled Wilbur to the ground. "We'll have to fish or cut bait," I said. Sometimes a girl's gotta' do what a girl's gotta' do. Turning into Hercules, I yanked the hook out of Wilbur's tongue as quickly and painlessly as possible. Elmer left town, fearing he might be next. Sparky lay by my side, seeming to say, "I didn't do it." Wilbur stopped squealing immediately and wanted to know what's for dinner.

"We can have fillet 'o Wilbur," I suggested.

"I'm calling one of those TV fishing shows!" Ludwig said, excitedly.

"And I'm calling everybody for shore lunch. Our fresh catch of the day is pork tenderloin sandwiches."

• • •

"Away in a manger, no crib for a bed . . . the little Lord Jesus lay down his sweet head."

Christmastime on the farm is a favorite time of year.

Christmas brings it all home and reminds us of who we really are. It is a time for farmers to count their blessings. Crops are in, animals are wintered down and big pots of bountiful harvest simmer on the stove.

Ludwig burst through the backdoor, wearing his tan, Carhartt bib overalls. "My word, it's cold out there! It's fifteen below!"

Stirring a pot of soup, I turned to face him. I couldn't see his face. He looked like a cherry popsicle. Ludwig's eyebrows sported icicles dangling to his nose. His mustache was frozen to his lips. His mustache had grown two inches.

"It looks like you've been climbing Mt. Everest," I told him.

The phone rang.

"Hi, Callie, this is Holly from Green Acres Country Club. Remember us?"

"Well, hello, stranger!" I replied. "How are things in the city?"

"Everything's the same. Well, our dinner menu changed a little. We now have your lobster special every Friday," Holly laughed.

Ah, the good old days. Surf and turf. Networking over lunch. Paying an arm and a leg for a golf membership.

"We were wondering if we could get you people to come on down to the city for a special Christmas event," Holly said. "You know how we like to do something different each year."

The thought of donning an evening gown startled me. I glanced at Ludwig and tried to imagine him dressed in a tux. My James Bond sat at the kitchen table soaking frostbitten feet in a tub of cool water.

"All three of you are invited as our special guests, but we do have one request. Someone told us that you have pot-bellied pigs."

Elmer, Wilbur and Sparky laid curled up with each

other next to the wood stove. "Why, yes, we have pigs," I laughed. "What's the request?"

"We were wondering if you could bring them in for our nativity scene. We want to have live animals this year. We think the kids will really enjoy it."

"Sure!" I replied without thinking. It did not dawn on me at the time that a pig just might be out of place in a nativity scene.

"Great," said Holly. "Then we'll see you next Saturday evening at six."

Next Saturday arrived quickly and thank goodness the weather lifted. Looking like we were off to the opera, the three of us hoisted Elmer and Wilbur into the back seat of the pickup. My black evening gown matched Ludwig's apparel nicely. PuLaRoo was absolutely lovely in her red velvet Christmas dress.

"I just love the Christmas parties at the Club!" Pu rejoiced. She said this while sitting in the backseat, attempting to keep Elmer and Wilbur in their seatbelts and off her party dress.

"And the Boys get to go to their first Christmas party!" I exclaimed.

Ten miles down the road, Pu demanded I switch places with her. "Elmer's wrecking my dress, Mom!"

Ludwig pulled over to the side of the road. Having changed places, Elmer demanded he sit on my lap. Wilbur satisfied himself with looking out the window. "We're never doing this again," I said.

I tried to stay calm, while sitting in the backseat of a pickup truck wearing a black evening gown with a pig on my lap. "We need to take a picture of this," I said dryly.

As we drove closer to the city, true amazement met us. We giggled. "Look at all the stop lights," we admired. "They look like Christmas lights!"

"Why, I haven't seen so many lights in so long. They're just beautiful," I sighed. "The whole city looks like a Christmas tree."

We came to a stop light and the people next to us pointed excitedly to our truck. Realizing I probably did look a little strange, sitting in the backseat with a pig on my lap, I smiled back. I held Elmer up to the window for effect.

The parking lot was jam-packed at Green Acres Country Club. The annual Christmas party is their biggest event of the year. "Come on, Boys," we said to Elmer and Wilbur. The Boys trotted dutifully behind us.

"We have a special spot for your little friends," Holly informed us. "The nativity scene is in the back, close by the windows so that everyone can see."

What a beautiful manger scene. Approximating the eastern star, red and green lights softly flooded the wooden shelter. Three life-sized, glittery, hand-painted Magi, stood to the left, bearing gifts of gold, frankincense, and myrrh.

Always willing to share the true meaning of Christmas, I quoted, "All this took place to fulfill what the Lord had said through the prophet: 'The virgin will be with child and will give birth to a son, and they will call him Immanuel--which means, 'God with us.'"

Two hand-painted shepherd statues stood to the right of the manger. Two children, dressed as Mary and Joseph, knelt in a mound of straw before the manger. The children were to take turns, so that all could play Mary and Joseph. A plastic baby doll wrapped in swaddling cloths played Immanuel, the Baby Jesus. Elmer and Wilbur were not the only live animals. The Club had rented a lamb and a donkey. Apparently exhausted from their Christmas tour, the lamb and donkey slept in soft mounds of straw. I handed Mary and Joseph a plate of ginger snaps for Elmer and Wilbur.

"We'll be right inside, if you need us," I told the children. "Elmer and Wilbur should be just fine, if you keep feeding them ginger snaps. If they get restless, they like their tummies rubbed."

Inside, I tried to stand up straight in my evening gown. Ludwig joined his old golfing buddies. As they gathered around him, Ludwig excitedly told them about his new manure spreader.

I missed my sweat-pants and long underwear. Going out to dinner in our farm community meant changing into a clean flannel shirt. My feet, quite used to muck boots by now, teetered two inches above-ground in high heels.

Glad to finally sit down and give my feet a rest, I took my place with Ludwig and Pu at a window table. As I glanced at the manger scene, I saw Wilbur and Elmer devour ginger snaps, along with Mary and Joseph.

"Just relax," said Ludwig. "Enjoy yourself,"

"Yeah, Mom, relax."

"I hope Elmer and Wilbur will be okay," I replied.

Elmer and Wilbur were a.o.k. It was the manger scene that was in jeopardy. The dining room chatter intensified as people stared astonished at Elmer, scratching himself against the tallest Magi. Elmer loves a good hinie scratch.

"Uh oh," I said.

The tallest of the three Magi, lined in a row, rocked back and forth to Elmer's rhythm. Realizing a potential Magi domino effect, I frantically knocked on the window and motioned for Mary and Joseph to remove themselves immediately.

Mary and Joseph scurried away just in time, as the three Magi crashed to the ground one on top of the other. Out of ginger snaps, Elmer and Wilbur thought the Savior just might make a good snack. Using his snout, Elmer flung the manger to its side while Wilbur snatched Baby Jesus.

The shepherds stood by "in the fields nearby, keeping watch over their flocks by night."

The dining-room management did not "keep watch over their flock." They rushed out the door to try to save what was left of their expensive manger scene. Elmer and Wilbur grew upset with the commotion and hustled out through the shepherds keeping watch.

The shepherds awakened the sleeping donkey by landing on top of him. Both donkey and lamb bolted for the eighteenth green. The Club President attempted to pry the Baby Jesus doll out of Wilbur's mouth.

Right on the heels of the Club attorneys, I hollered, "Let go of Baby Jesus, Wilbur!"

Having none of it, Wilbur took off with Immanuel.

A man in a tux whispered into a walkie-talkie, "Get Club Security."

Elmer followed Wilbur, and the two of them dashed down the driveway, past the club security entrance. The man in the tux whispered again into the walkie-talkie, "The pig has Baby Jesus."

Club management called the city police. A squad car drove up with a canine. In a frenzy, I told the officer, "You can't send a dog after pigs. The dog will eat the pigs."

"Then what do you suggest we do, lady?"

He thought for a moment and added, "We'll have to do a neighborhood search. We just passed some carolers on the way in, maybe they'll help."

Glad to be pig-spotters, the carolers eagerly went door to door. The only problem was that people answering their doors did not quite understand what, "Hark the Herald Angels Sing," had to do with pigs.

Fearing that a curse might indeed be upon us, I hopefully looked up into the clear night sky and asked, "Where are Elmer and Wilbur?"

Just then, a little caroler whispered in my ear, "Maybe we should check the nativity scene down by the McGees."

Following the little boy, whom I later dubbed my "eastern star," we pranced our red noses down the block. Lo and behold, there lay Elmer and Wilbur snuggled in swaddling cloths. Stealing a second Immanuel from the McGee's manger, Elmer and Wilbur had expertly wrapped the doll's swaddling blanket around their backs for warmth.

Away in a Manger, "The little Lord Jesus laid down his sweet head . . . " Elmer and Wilbur snored as they each rested upon a Baby Jesus pillow.

Overcome by relief, I stared down at Elmer and Wilbur and remembered a grownup Jesus saying, ""Come to me, all you who are weary and burdened, and I will give you rest.'"

Elmer and Wilbur rested in all their glory for about two seconds. The evening did not turn out to be a "Silent Night." Elmer and Wilbur decided to head back to "O Little Town of Bethlehem," and the Merry Gentlemen followed behind.

Chapter Six

Current Jam

I knew it was cold when I could not pry my nostrils apart. Living on a farm presents its own challenges. For instance, animals must eat, and somebody has to feed them.

"Who's going to feed the horses and the chickens?" I asked somebody.

"Mom, we can't even see out the windows," said Pu.

"Just pretend you're at Dr. Zhivago's dacha, Pu," I told her. "At least we don't have to make that long, horrible trek across Russia."

I spoke too soon. Ludwig and I had to make a horrible hike out to the barn. The temperature had hit thirty-seven degrees below zero. The wind chill factor came in at fifty-three below zero.

I colorfully draped blankets and sheets over the windows. Perhaps draping them isn't the right word. I nailed them to the window frames. Adding an extra layer can sometimes make a difference.

The weatherman on TV chirped, "Stay inside today. Bare skin will freeze within seconds."

Obviously, he was not talking to us, or to the farmers in the surrounding area. "Go outside only if you have an emergency," the weatherman continued.

"Does feeding Little Mel come under an 'emergency,' Ludwig?" I asked. "It does if you break your neck on the ice," he offered.

I drew a blanket back from a window and peeked outside. It looked barren and uninhabitable. "I just don't know how the farmers do it," I said.

I had now observed spring planting, harvesting, and winter. Our neighbors usually began work at five in the morning and tractors could hum well past midnight. I asked our neighbor, Earl, "Why do you do this?"

"Because I'm my own boss," Earl replied, "I'm a meteorologist, chemist, accountant, veterinarian, Ag specialist, inventor and a professional gambler."

"Right," I told him, "Who needs Vegas when you can gamble on nature?"

"Besides, it's in my blood and the pay is good . . . about fifty cents an hour," he added.

I hoped my blood was circulating properly, as I clothed myself in layer-upon-layer to brave the cold. Ludwig and I looked like we were going on a spacewalk.

"Are you ready for this?" he asked.

"Ready as I'll ever be," I replied.

The snow was so cold that it crumbled into crystals beneath our feet. The horses, Animal and Sam, stood in their stalls with frost covering their winter coats. Horses and other animals grow winter coats, not according to dropping temperatures, but in response to sunlight. As the days get shorter, the coats get longer. The days were now as short as our bank account.

"Can't put them outside today," said Ludwig, "The wind chill will get them."

"I wonder how Earl's cows are getting along?"

Cows are not usually put in stalls unless they're milkers. Cows have to stand outside and just take it. They cluster themselves to break the wind.

"At least they have hides, Callie," he replied. "But I know what you mean. Hope they come through it."

Ludwig said this as he tried to pump water. "The water hydrant is frozen solid."

"Oh, great. What does that mean?" I asked through my scarf.

"It means the cold drove the frost down. It probably won't thaw until spring."

Horses can drink a good ten gallons or more a day. How to get water to the horses and chickens became the next trick. Believe me, after our first winter, I no longer took running water for granted.

"We can't run a hose from the house. It's too far," Ludwig said.

He said this through a mouth that didn't operate correctly. We could hardly take a breath through the cold. Our lungs froze.

"We'll transport buckets from the house. I'll have to bring in a hundred-gallon water tank from the pasture. While I try to chisel it out of the snow, you'll have to run into town and pick up a tank heater."

We stumbled through the cold back to the house. Pu sat snuggled in a blanket, watching TV.

"They're warning everybody not to go outside," she said. "Are the horses okay? How are the chickens?"

"Everybody's fine. The chickens made tunnels through the hay bales," I answered.

"Roberta called. She wants you to call her back."

Returning my city friend's call, I said, "Hi, Roberta! I only have a minute to talk. Our water pump is frozen!"

"We were just wondering how you're doing out there. Are you sure you don't want to move back to the city?"

"No, I just love it out here," I replied, not entirely sure of my answer. "What are you doing?"

"The kids have the day off, and we have a fire going in the fireplace. We just rented some great movies. The pizza should be here any minute."

"Pizza delivery?" I asked, green with envy.

Our closest pizza delivery is forty miles away. "We'll probably watch a video later," I told her. "We'll watch 'Journey Into No Man's Land.'

"You take care of yourselves out there. We worry about you."

"Thanks, Roberta, we're fine. I'm glad for indoor plumbing." And I truly meant it.

Bidding Roberta farewell, as well as Pu and Ludwig, I was off to the feed store for the tank heater. The town of Waterdale lies only a short distance away. Ten miles is considered a hop, skip, and a jump. With a population of nine hundred, it's easy to find a parking space.

A trip to the local grain mill/feed store is an experience in itself. The store is a gathering place for local farmers. Women are certainly welcome, but there must be a reason the entire store came to a hush the moment I walked through the door.

We have been observed with amusement ever since our arrival on the farm scene. One is considered a newcomer if one has only lived on a particular farm for twenty years. I wiped off my lipstick before entering.

"Hi, Chuck!" I exclaimed gruffly, trying to blend in with the boys. I expected my visits added fodder to cafe conversations. Every day local farmers gather for lunch at Kathy's Kafe. Ludwig and I call it the Plugged Artery. Kathy is a "Butter Believer."

"I need something called a tank heater," I told Chuck.

Two farmers, sitting on a wooden display table, wearing layers of Carhartts, bent their ears.

"How are you folks doing out there?" asked Leroy, the pig farmer. "Think you'll make it through your first winter?"

Pretending not to be a wimp, I said, "We're doing pretty well, but it sure is nippy. The barn hydrant froze."

Three heads nodded in sage agreement. "We're frozen too," said a weathered face. "Won't thaw until spring. I have a hundred cows sitting out there. Can't get the round bales off the field, either."

At least I knew what a round bale of hay was, and I shook my head in sympathy. "And you guys do this every year," I said.

Chuck poked Leroy. "But we love it. Don't we, Leroy?"

The boys jostled manfully for a moment, and Leroy spit tobacco on the floor.

"Callie's got them pot-bellied pigs, Leroy," said Chuck. "She keeps them in the house."

This brought an uproar from the farming community.

"It's a little cold for them fellas to go outside, if you know what I mean," laughed Leroy. "But, believe me, we've had our share of pig litters in the kitchen."

"Thank goodness we don't have a litter, but we sure do have a big litter box. We had to bring in a kid's swimming pool and fill it with sand. It's in the middle of the living room," I informed them.

"Try raising calves in the basement," laughed Floyd, the cattle farmer. "My wife hates it when I bring an orphan in the house. Calves won't use a litter box!"

"So, how are you going to get water to the barn?" asked Chuck.

"I think we'll have to carry it," I grimaced.

"Them buckets weigh fifty pounds apiece. Think you can handle it?" asked Leroy.

"I don't need the health club anymore, Leroy. Take a look at this."

I stuck out my arm and pointed to the muscle. "Just feel this."

The boys gathered round, thinking this pretty darned interesting.

"She's got muscle, all right," Leroy reported to the bunch. "And it's a big one."

"Better not mess with you, huh, Callie?" asked Chuck.

"And I'm getting pretty good at cracking the whip, too," I laughed.

"Oh, you mean making the hubby do the chores," said Floyd raising his eyebrows theatrically.

"No, I mean a real whip. You have to use a whip for lunging. You know, exercising the horse, making them run around in circles . . . "

Farmer eyes widened. Thinking they found my whip cracking extremely impressive, I went on. "It's all in the wrist. You have to snap it."

I demonstrated my whip snapping technique in the air.

"Ouch!" yelled Leroy.

"You don't hit the horse with it, Leroy, you snap at the air behind the horse."

"Uh huh," said a pair of even wider eyes.

"No doubt about it. It looks like she can use a whip," agreed Chuck.

I grew suspicious and realized my audience was too attentive. Their eyes had too many twinkles. Best to pull a disappearing act, I decided.

"Oh, my, look at the time," I said glancing at the overhead clock. "I have to get that tank heater! Ludwig's waiting!"

"Just don't take the whip to him," Leroy laughed while slapping his knee.

I rolled my eyes in embarrassment and walked out with the tank heater.

• • •

Back home, Ludwig and Pu met me at the door. I took one look at their faces and asked, "What's wrong?"

"It's one of the chickens, Mom," said Pu.

Pu started to cry.

"Is it Little Mel?" I asked.

"No, it's Pu-Two," PuLaRoo said through her tears. "She's dead."

"Oh, no . . . how did she die?"

"We don't know, we think Sparky . . . " Pu said pausing, "killed her."

"Our Sparky?" I asked in amazement.

"Sparky was outside, and she brought Pu-Two to the backdoor."

"We'll have to do something," said Ludwig. "Once a dog kills a chicken, they say it's only the first."

"Let me call Chuck and see if he has any suggestions," I answered.

Chuck answered the phone, and I heard uproarious laughter in the background. "You have to snap it like this," I heard someone say.

Still flustered over my obvious mistake in doing a whip snapping demonstration, I managed to tell Chuck about our incident.

"You have to shame the dog, Callie," Chuck told me. "You have to isolate the dog. What we do is to tie the chicken around the dog's neck."

"Are you kidding me?" I asked Chuck. "Is this for real?"

He laughed, "No. I'm not kidding! You have to scold them and put the chicken in their face. It worked for us."

I relayed the information to Ludwig and Pu.

"We can put electric heaters in the tack room and put Sparky in there for a while," said Ludwig.

Sparky got a good scolding, and we tied Pu-Two around Sparky's neck with twine. With a black feather boa chicken around her neck, Sparky looked as though she were ready to go out for the evening. Sparky was banished to the tack room with Pu-Two as her date.

We gave Sparky about an hour of shamefulness and went to check on her. Pu-Two no longer adorned the wonder dog. Feathers lay scattered, and two tan chicken feet hung from Sparky's twine necklace like charms.

"I can't believe this," I told Ludwig. "Did Sparky eat

Pu-Two?"

Ludwig and I stared at the hanging chicken feet in absolute disbelief. Sparky blinked back at us looking grateful for the unusual treat.

"She ate her all right. And it looks like Sparky loves frozen chicken dinners. Next thing you know, she'll want a pot pie," said Ludwig.

We returned to the house with our shameful dog to find Pu at the door.

"Chuck just called. He said that one of the farmers lost chickens today, too. Said they died of heart attacks from the weather."

We were very pleased to learn that Pu-Two probably died of natural causes, and we apologized to Sparky. We held a memorial service for Pu-Two that evening. Pu keeps Pu-Two's little feet inside a box on her dresser and takes them out on special occasions.

• • •

A few weeks later, I almost died of a heart attack when I opened the electric bill. "Four-hundred and thirty-one dollars!" I shouted.

In not being accustomed to working outside ten hours a day in sub-zero temperatures, Ludwig and I carry electric heaters wherever we go. Our electricity consumption caught us by surprise.

A helicopter flying over the house also caught me by surprise.

"They must be doing maneuvers," I said running to the window.

The helicopter appeared to circle the property. Standing on the back stoop, I waved to the pilot.

"They probably think our property is really neat to fly over," I told Pu. "They must like to look at the horses in the pasture."

When Ludwig returned home from work, I told him about the unusual helicopter citing. Army cargo planes flew overhead on occasion, and I figured we were in a flight pattern.

"You don't think they're spying on us from up there, do you, Ludwig?" I asked.

"Are you sure it was Army?" he answered. "The Army doesn't spy. Was it a green helicopter?"

"No, but it had a dark color to it. Maybe it's from the little airport over by Browntown."

Trying to dismiss spying helicopter thoughts, I quickly switched over to worrying about the electric bill.

"I'd better call the electric company and complain," I told Ludwig.

"See if you can get it reduced," he said. "They must have made a mistake."

"This is Mrs. Carlson at . . ."

"On Rural Route Three?" a voice said before I could finish.

"How did you know?" I asked the stranger.

"You're red-flagged," said a male voice.

"Oh, you mean because of our electric bill?"

"You have a pretty high bill this month, Mrs. Carlson."

"Well, don't I know it!" I told him.

"We were wondering if we could send some people out there to check and see why it's so high."

"You mean like come out and see how we can reduce the bill?" I asked.

"Yes, something like that," he replied.

"Do you know when you'll be coming?"

"Oh, we'll get out there sometime today," he responded.

"Great! We'll see you when you get here," I said.

I woke Ludwig up from his snooze on the couch.

"I can't believe how nice everybody is out here," I told Ludwig. "The electric company is going to send someone out today to help us."

An hour later a dark-colored car drove up the driveway. Two men got out of the car, and they wore identical jackets.

"Do you think they're in a gang?" I asked Ludwig, while watching nervously out the window.

"No, I don't think it's a gang, Callie," replied Ludwig, "It looks official. They have initials on the back of their jackets."

"Are they in a bowling league?"

"Don't think so, it starts with a letter P," Ludwig said straining to see. "Callie, it's the police."

I made a beeline for the door, wondering if they would try to flush us out.

"Walk very slowly, Callie," Ludwig told me. "Let them see your hands at all times. They mean business."

"Oh, my word, Ludwig! I can't believe this!"

The men approached the house minus their guns drawn. I stood on the back stoop shaking like a leaf.

"Good afternoon, Mr. and Mrs. Carlson," said one of the men.

"And a good afternoon to you," replied Ludwig.

"Do you mind if we take a look around?" he asked.

"Can we ask what you're looking for?" asked Ludwig.

"Pot," one of the men snapped.

"Pot? You mean marijuana?" I asked in amazement. "Why, I don't even listen to rock and roll music!"

"We just need to make sure. We'll just look around the buildings if you don't mind."

"It's all right, Callie," Ludwig reassured me, "I think they have to separate us while they're looking."

Ludwig went inside the house with one man, and I treated the other one to a personal tour of the farm.

"Why on earth would you think we have marijuana?" I asked as I took him to the barn.

"A big electric bill that jumps like yours did, tells us something, Mrs. Carlson."

When we arrived at the barn, he hesitated before entering.

"It's fine. Come on in," I told him.

I snapped on the overhead lights and nothing happened.

"Just great. Did they just turn off our electricity?" I asked.

Suddenly the policeman twitched into an attack pose.

"What's that rustling noise?" he asked. "It's coming from behind those hay bales."

"How many people do you have out here, Mrs. Carlson?" he blurted.

"Ah . . . I think it might be Elmer and Wilbur," I responded.

"Elmer and Wilbur work for you, do they?"

"Well . . . they don't exactly do any work. They just lie around most of the time."

"Hard to find good help, is it?"

"Well, yes, actually it is. I keep advertising in the local paper. We pay above minimum wage, but we still can't get the kids to come out here and work."

"You've tried to enlist children?" he exclaimed.

"Well, I tried, but it hasn't worked. We have to do all the work ourselves."

"Let's get Elmer and Wilbur out here right now," he insisted.

"Let's go!" he shouted at the hay bales.

"They won't come out if you yell at them," I huffed.

The rustling grew louder, and Elmer must have panicked.

Stuck behind a hay bale, he let out one of his blood curdling squeals. Wilbur joined him in chorus. Squeals reverberated throughout the metal building.

"Pigs!" he shouted. He covered his ears and ran out of the barn.

Outside, we both rubbed our ears.

"I have to live with this on a daily basis," I tried to explain.

"We'll get your electricity turned back on," he said, suddenly apologetically. "Just watch your electric consumption in the future. A sudden increase as big as yours triggers an investigation. We had to see if you had a hot-house going."

"A hot-house?" I asked. "You mean like a greenhouse? I was thinking of putting one in . . . "

"I don't mean for vegetables and roses, Mrs. Carlson,"

he laughed. "Never mind."

Not only are we adding fodder to Kathy's Kafe a.k.a. the Plugged Artery, we are now the talk of the electric company and the county court house.

News travels fast. We seem to be linked to a satellite dish. It seems our escapades are being beamed into rural living rooms for nightly entertainment.

When Ludwig accidently drove the tractor off the driveway, the next day at the hardware store, Dovie asked, "Hey, did you get your tractor out?"

I answered, "Yes, Dovie. Thank you. Thank you for your concern. It's nice to have so many guardian angels."

"Well, we worry about you, being so new and all. Leroy was going to come pull you out. You take care, now, you hear?"

"Thanks, Dovie," I said, "Say, how much do those satellite dishes cost, anyway?"

We miss CNN.

Chapter Seven

I Shall Fear No Cows

Norwegian bachelor farmers really do exist. I met them in the coffee section at the grocery store. A Norwegian out of coffee or a pound of butter is not a pretty sight.

Both dressed in tan, Carhartt bib overalls, Larry and Del argued softly among themselves.

"Yah, you're crazy if you tink I'm going to drink dat fancy, smansie coffee," whispered Bachelor Number One.

Disgruntled Norwegians do not shout. They complain to one another sotto voce. Bachelor Number Two, the coffee bean connoisseur, wished to expand into hazelnut.

"Let's yust try it," pleaded Del.

Larry refused to take part in coffee blasphemy.

"Yah, sure," replied Del, "you never try anyting new."

Larry and Del broke away from their whispered argument. "Yah, let's yust ask dis lady," Larry said pointing to me. "Vat do you tink?"

"Why don't you compromise and try a mixed blend?" I offered while scrounging around in the noodle section.

"She drinks dat Latte Da coffee," Larry whispered to Del. They looked me up and down. My tight leggings and faux fur coat seemed out of place. Del's curiosity got the better of him. "Yah, say, aren't you da nutecomers out on Route Tree?" asked Del.

"Yes. That would be us," I acknowledged.

Once a nutecomer, always a nutecomer. "Hey, yah sure, mind if ve stop in some day and take a look around? Heard dat you've done quite a bit of vork to da old place," said Larry, while scratching industrially under his Carhartt cap.

Being Norwegian myself, I replied cheerfully, "Yah, sure, come on by. Everybody else does."

One thing about living in the country is that people stop by to visit, no matter what time of day it is or what day. Except Sundays. Sundays are reserved for God and family. I always find it amazing that a town of nine hundred has twenty churches within a ten-mile radius.

I also find it amazing that I must be showered by five-thirty in the morning. On many occasions, I have looked out into the dark of night and spotted clusters of cars in our driveway.

Waking Ludwig out of a deep sleep, I asked, "Why are the workmen staring up at our bathroom window?"

Ludwig rolled over and said, "They're waiting for you to turn on the light. They want to get started."

Country workmen arise at four-thirty and try to arrive at their destinations by five-thirty a.m. There are two reasons for this early bird special. Hunting and fishing.

Even the town of Waterdale keeps odd hours. The post office and bank are open from ten until one. After lunch, they reopen at two and close at three. They are not open on Saturdays.

Imagine my surprise when I looked out the window to see Larry and Del moseying up our driveway at six in the morning on Saturday. Dressed in matching tan, Carhartt overalls and Carhartt hats, they reminded me of nothing so much as the Bobbsey Twins.

"Is Ludwig home?" they asked in unison.

"Ludwig is still in bed," I replied, "but he'll be down in a few minutes. Coffee?"

Previously unaccustomed to unannounced arrivals, Ludwig and I usually imagine an emergency at hand when someone shows up at the door. We think to ourselves, "What is the reason for this visit? Surely, something is awry." It never dawns on us that people actually stop by at six a.m. to chat.

Chatting is a farmer ritual. Farmers visit one another. Farmers spend hours shuffling their feet in the dust while assessing one another's equipment and yields. Wives usually stay in the house and ponder these inspections through windows.

Alfalfa inspection appears to be a historical favorite. Alfalfa is tasted, smelled, and scrunched up in worn-out, weather-crackled hands. Laboratory reports on alfalfa are not necessary. A good farmer can tell the moisture content, protein level, exact seed mix, and point of origin. We discovered our alfalfa originates in a swamp.

"Yah, you got taken," Larry said, shaking his head at Ludwig.

Del chuckled. "Yah, you must have got your hay from dat Yimmie."

"Yah, this is svamp grass," said Larry, the bearer of bad news. "Don't vorry, ve'll get you some real alfalfa. Ve'll even trow in a few cows to go vit it. It's time you started your own herd."

Ludwig's eyes lit up like moon rockets. Light-bulbs went off over his head. "Cows? Cows . . . ," he said, dreamily.

Ludwig returned to the house a cattle rancher.

"Have you heard about the herd?" he asked, excitedly. "We'll start out small. Larry and Del are going to deliver three cows to us this afternoon."

Pu walked into the kitchen, wiping the sleep out of her eyes.

"Did I hear you say cows? We're getting some cows? Cool!" said Pu.

"Guess so!" I replied. "Daddy is buying us some cows!"

"And!" he said excitedly, "They're all pregnant! We'll be calving this spring!"

"Calving? Ludwig, do we know how to calve? What do we have to do for calving?"

"Absolutely nothing. The cow does it. Cows have calves all the time, Callie! They're used to it," he smiled, smugly.

That afternoon Larry returned with a stock trailer full of pregnant cows. Del rattled close behind with a hay wagon overflowing in alfalfa.

"Yah, dis is for da cows, and I'll bring over a good horse mix later," said Del. "Horse hay needs to be a mix of alfalfa and grass."

The farmer before us raised beef cattle, so our farm was already set up with a cattle shed and a fenced paddock. Our excitement level for our new cattle venture rated high.

However, I considered cows to be your basic large pet. Larry backed the trailer up to an open gate in the paddock. I expected the cows to peek out, take a look around, and maybe greet their new owners.

"STAND CLEAR!" shouted Larry. "CHUTE OPENING!"

A cattle stampede shot out the door. Our new black Angus cows, Flower, Margie, and Henrietta galloped the fence line. Lunging this way and that, it felt like we were in Pamplona at the running of the bulls.

"Don't vorry, da girls vill get used to the place," said Larry.

We all watched as the girls trampled the pasture.

"Yust don't go near them for a few days," said Larry. "Dey need time to a-yust."

"Yah sure, de'll settle in," Del reassured us.

"But now, vat you really need is a bull," Larry decided.

"Excuse me," I said, "but if the cows are already going to have babies, why do we need a bull?"

"Because you'll vant more 'babies,'" laughed Del. "Velcomen to farming!"

I don't know how velcomened I felt. The girls didn't even say hi as they flew past. I am their new mom, after all.

• • •

When Saturday morning rolled around, our house awoke to hyperactivity. As I glanced into the living room, I saw three little heads poking out from sleeping bags.

"Is it time yet, Callie?" one of the little boys asked. "Is it time to get the bull?"

Our little second grade visitor looked innocent enough, which made it hard to believe that others considered him an ADD terrorist. Corky can be a handful at school, and on too many occasions, the neighborhood bully. And while experts often disagree on Attention Deficit Disorder conclusions, I have no doubt it is proper in Corky's case.

Ludwig and I have always had special spots in our hearts for little boys who can't sit still. We did not actively pursue volunteerism in the hyperactivity area, it simply happened. Early on in our marriage, little boys began to appear on our doorstep.

It all began when a four-year-old stood on our steps one day with a plastic guitar in hand and asked, "Can Ludwig come out and play?"

Gazing down on a little blonde head of hair, I called to Ludwig, "You have a visitor!"

We called him "The Singer."

Children gravitate to Ludwig. The Singer and Ludwig would sit in our big arm chair for hours and compose songs. Ludwig was also known as the neighborhood bike rider, and was always game for a trip to the local jungle gym with Pu and friends. Ludwig is the only man alive willing to ride his ten-speed with playing cards clothes-pinned to his spokes.

By now, our home was growing into a haven of sorts for boys just like Corky. Boys with ADD seemed to materialize from out of the cornfields. It made for a busy household at times.

And word spread. Mothers contacted us when they needed a well-deserved break. "Can you take my son for the day?" they often pleaded.

Our little visitors briefly resembled angels.

"We'll go in a few hours," I replied. "Did you get some sleep?"

Corky crawled out of his sleeping bag and gave me an unexpected hug.

"I just love it out here, Callie," he said, looking up at me earnestly.

"I know you do, Corky. We're glad to have you here," I said to the second grader.

I don't know when it happened, but my view of life went through a catharsis. I used to be an uptight mother, fretting over clowns and catered affairs for Pu's birthday parties. Children called me "Mrs. Carlson" and our all-white living room was as perfect as a museum piece.

We still have the same furniture; expensive white couches, black ebony dining-room set, and a black polished baby grand piano to match. But now, we actually use them.

Bouncing around on a farm is an attractive sport for a child with ADD. Having very short attention spans, they can switch from one farm activity to the next in seconds flat. Pounding nails into random boards seems to be the favorite activity.

Ludwig and I went out and bought lumber, nails, and hammers. We told the boys, "Pick a tree. Go make yourselves a tree-house." We have an ongoing, never to be finished, tree house project.

We found used bicycles at garage sales. We put up a basketball hoop in the driveway. We built a fire-pit. I am the marshmallow, hot dog queen of the county.

At Callie's house, little boys are allowed to play with fire. Little boys are transformed into kings at bonfires.

Marching to their own drummers, they carry their glowing corn stalks like royal scepters. Pocket knives are not confiscated, they are used for whittling marshmallow sticks and carving letters on trees. And best of all, you don't have to come in when it gets dark. That's when the fun begins.

"Can we play flashlight tonight?" asked Corky. "Can we run through the woods and you try to find us, huh, Callie?"

"Sure," I said laughing, knowing full well they wouldn't go far. After all, it's too scary out there.

Sleepy heads walked into the kitchen. Three little boys asked if it was time to brush their teeth again. I laughed, "We need to brush our teeth after breakfast, remember?"

They argued over who got to set the table. Butch, a third grader, piped up, "Now, we don't just grab at the food, right, Callie?" he said, looking pointedly at the others. Butch was obviously very proud of himself and wanted the others to acknowledge his authority. "You have to ask the person next to you to pass it, right, Callie?"

"Right-o, Butch, you got it," I replied. "You sure do remember well, don't you?"

He grinned, and nodded. "I sure do," he replied.

Not to be outdone by Butch's impressive etiquette review, Corky added, "And we say a prayer before we eat, don't we, Callie?"

"Yep, at this house we do," I said smiling. "Do you remember it?"

Corky winced and said slowly, "Come Lord Jesus be our guest, let these gifts to us be messed."

I burst out laughing. "Very good, Corky, but it's blessed, not messed."

"Will you make your special eggs, Callie?" asked Chris, the oldest of the bunch. "You know the ones with the little onions and parsley in them?"

"Sure can! Glad you like them!" My cooking habits now require volume. Small portions have given way to huge pots of something or other simmering on the stove at all times. I tend to cook a lot of spaghetti, chili, and every kind of soup imaginable. Ludwig and Pu call it, "Callie's Soup Kitchen."

Callie's Soup Kitchen segued into "Alfalfabit Soup," hence, the name of our farm. This is due to the fact alfalfa "bits" become airborne, float through the air, and land in my soup. Ludwig is an "Alfalfa Carrier," meaning alfalfa particles stick to him like velcro. These particles, or "alfalfa-bits," have the ability to travel great distances. Everybody thinks I cook with parsley.

For a big breakfast crowd, huge mounds of scrambled eggs fit the bill. The "Callie Special" is scrambled eggs with chopped onions, cheese, and parsley. I won't tell if you won't tell. "Okay, everybody out while I cook breakfast. Go see what Ludwig is up to in the barn."

Three little farmers scooted out the door in their pajamas. It's not every day you get to sweep the barn in your pj's. The boys ran to the barn to play King of the Hill on the hay bales.

A few hours later, we were ready for our shopping spree. It's not every day you get to pick out your own bull. Larry and Del drove up the driveway. Our local bull experts. Surprised to see such a crowd for bull shopping, Larry looked at me and asked, "Yah, sure you vant to go vit us? Don't know yust how appropriate it is for a young lady," he said, looking at PuLaRoo.

"Hey, we're liberated women, aren't we, Pu?" I said.

We all piled into two pickups and made our way over to Hanson's Bull Farm. Breeding is his specialty. As we drove up, bulls dotted the countryside as far as the eye could see. We piled out of the trucks, amazed at the number.

"Yah sure, you got some real nice bulls here," Larry said to Hans Hanson.

Believe me, bull shopping brings out the cowboy in a man, it's better than a Macy's sale for women. The men ooed and awed over Hans Hanson's good fortune. Looking at bulls is even more exhilarating than looking at new tractors at an implement dealer.

"I rounded up some two and three-year olds for you," said Hans. "They're in the pen over here."

We all crowded along the paddock fence line. Our little visitors could hardly contain their excitement. Bull shopping is definitely a testosterone thing.

How much of a testosterone event, I had no idea. Larry pulled out a measuring tape from his pocket. The expression on his face was grave. Apparently, picking out a bull is serious business.

Larry looked at Pu and I, and was about to give us a run for our liberated money. Hans Hanson also pulled out a measuring tape from his pocket. Armed with their tapes, they opened the gate.

"Can we come in, too?" asked Butch.

"Yah sure," replied Hans. He looked at Pu and me,

and hesitantly waved us through the gate.

"Are you sure it's safe in here?" I asked, finding myself in the middle of ten bulls. "What about the children?"

"Oh, these bulls are fine," Hans told me, "It's when they get older that you have to watch your back."

"So, what are all the measuring tapes for?" I asked.

No one wanted to answer me. I looked at Ludwig and he shrugged, "Don't ask me."

Larry muttered something. "What, Larry? I can't hear you," I told him.

"Privates," he mumbled out of the corner of his mouth.

My brain wasn't functioning properly. "What did you say?" I asked again. "What's private?"

"His privates," he replied louder.

Three little boys giggled.

No one wanted to offer me an explanation.

Hans finally stepped in and reluctantly informed me, "A bull is judged by his circumference. It has to do with his performance level and breeding efficiency."

"Oh. I see," I replied, in sudden understanding. I silently wondered how many people knew about this.

This evoked massive giggling from the boys. They couldn't wait to get home and tell their schoolmates about this one. It sure beat a boring health class. Pu and I tried to pretend nothing in the world was wrong. Ludwig cringed.

"Which one do you want us to measure?" Hans asked Ludwig and me.

"They all look about the same to me," replied Ludwig. "I'm sure you can tell better than we can."

"How about that one over there?" I said, pointing to a bull in the corner.

"Ya sure, dat looks like a good one," said Del.

Never in a million years, I thought to myself. Never in a million years did I think I would be considering such things and be required to pick from out of a crowd.

Hans approached the bull with his tape measure.

"I'm sure they're . . . or I mean, he . . . is just fine," I said.

My face was as red as a ripe, old strawberry.

"Are you sure you don't want me to measure?" Hans asked in astonishment.

"Ludwig, do you want him to measure?" I asked.

Little boys continued to giggle in the background.

Ludwig laughed, "No, I'll let Callie pick this one. She probably knows what she's doing."

This precipitated thigh-slapping all around.

"Boy," I said, "I hope the feed store doesn't get wind of this one."

But, of course they did. Hans Hanson delivered our three-year-old bull that afternoon. Our little visitors named our new bull, Marty. Flower, Margie, and Henrietta bounced over to Marty and made friends instantly.

"I think Marty's looking forward to spring," said Ludwig.

"It looks like they all have twinkles in their eyes," I replied.

"Are they all married?" asked Corky.

Pu gave me a look that said, "How are you going to explain this one?"

Ludwig and I glanced sideways at each other, and

said, "They will be."

We quickly held a wedding ceremony, while we all hung over the fence. Corky was Best Man, and Pu, the Maid of Honor. Marty already had a ring in his nose.

Chapter Eight

One For the Road

Orville Johnson's brown UPS truck bounced up our driveway. Every time I see Orville, I think of Christmas. Playing Santa Claus in his brown, official UPS uniform, Orville comes bearing gifts of mail-orders. Mail-orders are an important aspect to living on a farm.

I love surprises. I always forget what I've ordered.

Orville is an extension of our family. Orville knows us better than our closest friends, because, I have realized, "You are what you order." Bless his heart, Orville is the perfect picture of *Best Service and Lower Rates.*

"Hi, Callie!" Orville shouted through his open UPS door. "How are you this fine day?"

"Great, Orville! And how are you and yours?"

"The Missus is going to visit relatives in Sveden, and the little ones have that flu bug that's going around."

Orville is my link to the outside world, and always brings me tidbits of welcome information. While watching the six o'clock news is all well and fine, Orville transmits more useful information, such as road conditions and what germs are making their way around the county.

"Say, you know those pot-bellied pigs of yours?" he asked. "One of our drivers has a pot-bellied pig and is looking for a good home."

"Looking for a good home," is a term often used in lieu of Animal Placement Services. Country folk have concocted their own solution to the Animal Humane

Society. The "looking for a good home," translation reads: "If you agree to take care of this animal, it's yours for free."

However, if one were to read the fine print beneath moving lips, one might discover, "This animal is driving me nuts, and I want to get rid of it."

"What's the deal, Orville?" I asked.

Midwesterners enjoy using the word "deal" to encompass a myriad of useful word combinations. It leaves any subject wide open to interpretation, allowing the responder to answer as he or she pleases.

"Kari-Marie has one lonely little pig over at her place. She wants to find a home where the pig will have company. I thought of you immediately," replied Orville.

Country folk know how to network. They do not need computers or telephones. Word of mouth has worked for hundreds of years, and it works just fine, thank you very much.

"Is it a boy or a girl?" I asked.

"Think it's a girl. Want Kari-Marie to stop by after work sometime?"

"Sure! Elmer and Wilbur will probably love a little sister."

Elmer and Wilbur began to spend much of their time outdoors. I built an elaborate straw hut for them in the barn, complete with reading lamps. Of course, they don't actually read the encyclopedia, but the light keeps them warm.

Elmer and Wilbur spent entire days rearranging their new apartment. Elmer took his role as interior decorator quite seriously. He searched the farm for any items not tied down and incorporated them into his motif.

It did not take long for Kari-Marie to contact us. She bounced up the driveway in her white pickup truck, and instead of delivering brown paper packages, she delivered Penny Pig.

Elmer and Wilbur were delighted. They thought Penny Pig extremely attractive and made room for her in their new apartment. Penny Pig relished all the attention and seemed to be as happy as a pig in a ginger snap pile. We simply did not understand her waywardness.

When days are quiet on the farm, it usually means something is about to happen. Ludwig went off to work, and Pu to school. When days are quiet, I sit at the kitchen table waiting for the other shoe to drop. Realizing that caffeine helps anxiety, I brewed another pot.

Ring-a-ling-a-ling.

"Hello?" I answered.

"Hi. Is this the Ludwig Carlson residence?" the voice asked.

"Yes, it is. This is Callie Carlson."

"Say, this is one of your neighbors, Marvin Swanson. Our place is probably about a mile west of you."

In the country, being a "neighbor" constitutes anyone within a seven-mile radius.

"Oh, hi. How are you today?"

At the time, I did not realize the significance of a telephone call. I thought Marvin called to chat. Farmers do not telephone to chat. They knock on your door to chat. Telephones are used to relay problems.

"Well, we heard you have those pot-bellied pigs . . . ," he said, his voice trailing off significantly.

"Yes, we have pigs . . . ," I responded

"I think one of them is down this way."

"What do you mean, down this way?" I asked.

"I saw a pig out on the highway," he replied.

"Well, you must be mistaken," I laughed. "It must be somebody else's pig. Our pigs are playing out in the yard."

"Well, just thought I'd call," he said.

"Okay, well, thanks for calling," I replied.

Out of curiosity I went outside. Sound asleep, Elmer and Wilbur lay snoring in their apartment. I started calling for Penny Pig and she was nowhere to be found. Suddenly frantic, I tried to remember Marvin's last name. Swanson. I reached for the phone and hoped he wasn't out on his tractor.

"Marvin! I think it is our pig! Where did you last see her?" I asked.

"She was on County Road Five headed west," he replied.

"Oh, great! How am I going to catch her?" I said, rising panic in my voice. Penny Pig wasn't exactly what one would call tame compared to Elmer and Wilbur. We were just getting to know each other.

"Well, I don't know exactly how you're going to catch her," Marvin replied.

"Marvin, I know you don't even know me, but do you think you can help?" I pleaded.

Marvin thought for a moment, then answered, "Yah, sure. I'll be over in a minute."

Everyone seems to know where the newcomers live. Upon hanging up, the phone rang again. Hoping it wasn't

Marvin changing his mind, I was afraid to answer.

"Is this the Ludwig Carlson residence?" asked a woman.

"Yes!" I practically shouted in her ear.

"I think I just saw your pig," she said.

"Where?" I said in my emergency voice.

"She's traveling down Soybean Lane. We think she's headed for the lake."

"Thank you so much for calling," I said, watching Marvin's blue pickup truck pull into the driveway.

Mind you, this put Penny Pig about two miles away from the house, apparently traveling at a record-breaking speed.

"Thank you so much for coming," I told Marvin.

"Yah, sure. Do you know how you're going to catch her?"

"I have no idea," I replied. "Do you have any suggestions? I'm new at this."

"Do you have any rope?"

We went to the barn and pulled it apart trying to locate anything that might assist in a pig capture.

"Let me run in the house and get some ginger snaps," I told Marvin.

"You're going to catch her with ginger snaps?" Marvin asked, surprised.

"I'm going to try," I attempted to smile.

As Marvin and I drove down the road in his blue pickup truck, we noticed a car pulled off to the side of the road. Animal rescue is a common occurrence in the country. Animals escape. If one happens to be on the road at the time and spots a wayward animal, it is one's job to pull over and point to the direction of the escapee. Words and conversations are not necessary, only an arm and a telling finger are required.

Marvin waved a farmer "thank you" as we drove past the car. The local "thank you," or "hello," for that matter, is done with just a slight tipping of an index finger. It may also include a simple, quarter-inch nod of a Carhartt hat.

Penny Pig had taken a detour, and if it hadn't been for the kind soul who stood at an intersection pointing, we never would have found her.

"I sure do appreciate this, Marvin," I told him.

"Yah, sure, we'll see," he said, "Let's see if we can catch her. Will she let you catch her?"

"Probably not," was my reply.

Penny Pig stood in the middle of an empty country road not even out of breath from her hike. She wasn't exactly glad to see us. Penny Pig preferred the open road. The only thing missing was a black leather jacket with an "Easy Rider" emblem.

"Throw some of those ginger snaps at her," offered Marvin.

Penny Pig seemed thrilled that I had packed her one for the road. Scarfing down ginger snaps, she looked expectantly for a baloney sandwich.

"Good, she's eating them," said Marvin. "Let me get the rope and make a lasso."

Fit to be tied, Penny Pig refused lassoing. Growing more frustrated with each swing of the rope, Marvin relinquished the lassoing to yours truly. Needless to say, I required practice for the rodeo.

"Let's try to make a trap with the rope," Marvin suggested.

We laid the rope on the ground and made a circle. We placed five ginger snaps inside its circumference. Penny Pig glared at us suspiciously. Not to be fooled by an obvious ginger snap trap, she snorted at us.

"If you think I'm going to step inside, you've got another thing coming," she seemed to say.

"Yah know, I hate to say this, but I have to get back to work," said Marvin.

"Can you suggest anything else?" I begged. "Please, Marvin, please?"

"Well, the only thing I can think of is to run her into a snowbank. Sometimes that works with cattle if you can get them stuck in a snowbank."

"Let's do it," I replied, enthusiasm itself.

Waving our arms and looking like lunatics, Marvin and I drove Penny Pig due north. Terrified by our behavior, she ran smack into a soybean field snowbank. Struggling to keep running, her short legs failed her.

"Sorry to tell you this, but I can't pick her up," Marvin told me. "I'm recuperating from back surgery."

Lifting a forty-pound pig out of a snowbank is a tall order for this mother. Especially since I got stuck in the process, along with Penny Pig. It's not like she had a suitcase handle attached to her back. I'd have to get under her in order to lift her. Once out of the snowbank, I wouldn't be able to put her down. We'd be back at square one. The entire feat seemed impossible.

Marvin stood helplessly at the side of the snowbank.

"Can't we call the Highway Patrol or something?" I

asked.

Marvin laughed. "No, we're pretty much on our own out here."

I pretended I was having a baby, but instead of pushing, I pulled. Penny Pig released and became airborne in my arms. With each step I took backward, I sank deeper into the snow. I felt like I was wearing fifty pounds of cement shoes. Penny Pig did not go quietly into the night, she struggled and squealed.

I never knew just how far twelve steps could take me. Twelve steps could take me to the blue pickup truck. "Today is the first day of the rest of your life." No, that's not it. "Each step is the first to . . . " No, that's not it either. How about, "One giant step for Callie, one small step for mankind." Penny Pig made a lunar landing in the back of the blue pickup truck. Head first, Moon Over the Midwest. I threw in a few ginger snaps for good measure.

Back home, I realized we had a new dilemma on our hands. Now that Penny Pig had tasted freedom and the open road, would she stay put? All the animals, except the horses and cows, are allowed to run free. But not that free. Sadly, I went to the telephone.

"Kari-Marie?" Thank goodness she was home.

"How's it going with Penny Pig?" she asked.

"Penny Pig is on the 'go' alright. She's decided to open up her own transport company. She transported herself as fast as her little hooves could hold the open road."

Karie-Marie laughed. "You mean you want an unofficial UPS pickup?" she laughed.

"Yes, I'm afraid so," I sighed.

"Look for my pickup in about twenty," she said.

"Thank you, Karie-Marie, I sure appreciate it."

"Hey," she laughed, "Always aim to please! *Best service, lowest rates,* you know!"

"And you are living proof," I added.

• • •

"Why can't I ride our horses?" asked PuLaRoo.

"They're so spirited, Pu. We're afraid you'll get hurt," I replied. "Besides, Animal needs training, he's never had a rider."

"We'll look around, Pu, and see if we can find you a good, safe, mount," offered Ludwig.

That week I went to the feed-store. Chuck sat alone behind his counter.

"Hi, Chuck," I said, "Do you happen to know of any good horses for sale?"

"Might just be, Callie. Take a look at the bulletin board."

Country folk love to be of service in animal procurement. I looked over the little slips of paper thumb-tacked to the wall. Sure enough, an ad for a Palomino horse caught my eye. My first thought? Trigger! We could have our very own Trigger!

I rushed home to wait for Ludwig and Pu's arrival. We flew into the pickup and fantasized excitedly about a Trigger lookalike. Trigger turned out to be a seventeen-year-old mare named Kizzy, a retired Endurance/Competitive Sport horse, who had seen more miles than the

Pony Express.

"Isn't she a bit old and worn out?" we asked.

"Oh, this girl can go forever," said Constance, our new horse friend. "I rode her for years in Competitive Riding."

"Is she safe for a young rider?" we asked.

"Kizzy came from a family with eight children. She taught my three boys to ride, and I suspect she'll be teaching my grandchildren."

Kizzy wasn't for sale exactly, she was to be on loan to the right family. Constance is unusual in that she is a person who enjoys promoting the sport of riding and is quite willing to give of herself and her horses, to the "right people," as she puts it. She took one look at Pu and decided Pu should learn how to ride Kizzy.

Of course, we thought this unusual, since it's not every day someone virtually gives you a horse. We did not look a gift horse in the mouth, we took Constance up on her offer. Kizzy came with one condition; Constance would visit from time to time to make sure we took good care of the mare.

"But, remember," Constance told us, "Kizzy is very smart. You have to keep an eye on her."

Kizzy got along fine with the geldings. Animal and Sam were glad to have the company and fought over who dated her. Our little herd of horses was well on its way. Pu popped a saddle on Kizzy the minute she arrived and began her trek toward riderhood.

• • •

I truly enjoy looking out the windows and watching the horses gallop through the pasture. In fact, I spend hours gazing out the window. When Ludwig comes home he asks, "What did you do today?" And I reply, "Looked out the window."

Spring finally sprung. Gazing out toward our woods, I could see the trees burst forth in their glorious spring palette. How ironic it was that our house blended perfectly with the scenery. A plausible paint salesman had definitely stopped by fifty years ago in the springtime. He must have talked many a farm family into going with the "lime-green to match the trees." We are not the only lime-green house in the neighborhood . . . they dot the countryside.

But alas, enough gazing out the window. Housework calls. Getting down to business, I got down on my hands and knees to scrub the kitchen floor. I don't know why I glanced up at the dining room window, but I did. I thought I saw a horse go by.

I could swear I saw Kizzy's head flash by, and I shook my head in disbelief. Animal's head appeared, then Sam's. Had I lost my mind?

To me, the most important piece of equipment on a farm is a gate. Apparently, we require deadbolts, because when I raced outside I found the horse-gate swinging wide open in the wind. Trigger-happy Kizzy was leading the pack.

Loose horses are a sight to behold. A breathtaking scene. Kizzy was herding the group through the alfalfa field, flying as free as the breeze. I cannot describe the panic that closed my throat. I was home alone. Again.

As it was springtime, I had hung our sheets out on the clothesline in the backyard. Kizzy decided a trip through the linens was in order. She is a smart one, all right. She thought it hilarious to whiz past me at full gallop. Animal wasn't so smart, as he negotiated the clothesline, draping a white sheet over his back as he flew through. This sparked panic in the herd, because everybody knows that a flapping white sheet is a ghost.

When horses are loose, all one can hope for is that they stick around. The week before, one of the farmers told me, he had found his cattle twenty miles away in the middle of a swamp. Penny Pig's flight was one thing, but a herd of loose horses is quite another.

Being new to the round-up business, I went to the barn to get their halters. We do not keep them on the horses when they're out in the pasture. Halters can snag on something/anything and be dangerous. It was foolish to think all three horses would stand still, let me put halters on them, and then allow me to lead them back through the gate.

Kizzy knew exactly what she was doing, but more importantly, she knew what I was doing. Obviously, this was not her first time on the free range. She looked at me sideways, observing my every move.

I held out an apple in my hand. Kizzy sidestepped nimbly, snatched it out of my hand and continued her tango around the yard. Ludwig and Pu weren't due home for another four hours. Could I hold out? I became an "endurance waiter."

Animal and Sam acted like a couple of dumb bunnies. Clearly, they didn't know what to do with their freedom, except to follow Kizzy. The only saving grace is they seemed to be staying on our land for the moment. Thank goodness, I discovered Penny Pig's county road map before they did.

I sat down on the stoop, terrified. A feeling of responsibility overwhelmed me. I am responsible for these animals, and there's nothing I can do about it.

"I wish I were back at the Mall!" I yelled into the air. At the Mall, I knew what to do with a herd of wild animals. "Give me a bargain sale any day!"

Sam and Animal inched toward me, fascinated by this strange woman yelling about Malls.

"Here, take it," I said, holding out an apple. "We've got a hot sale on freedom today."

I stood up, and Sam nuzzled his face in my hand, willing to taste the apple. Animal wanted his part, and he tried to jostle Sam over to eat it. Now, with two docile horses standing right in front of me, did I have a halter in hand? Of course not. Kizzy walked over to the three halters laying on the ground. She picked one up and swung it around and around in circles with her teeth. Sam and Animal nuzzled for more apples. Decisions, decisions. Do I grab the halter from Kizzy and try to put it on her, or do I try to halter Sam and Animal?

Now armed with two halters, I decided to go for Sam or Animal while Kizzy played with hers. Sam stood perfectly still as I buckled the halter. Animal, all of a sudden, wanted a halter too because Sam had one. Only, I didn't have any lead ropes attached to the halters in order to control them. I had to try to hold onto Sam's halter, while trying to also put one on Animal. I needed three or four hands.

Kizzy approached, looking for apples. Now I had all three horses available but not enough hands to go around. Where was Groucho Marx when I needed him? I finally got halters on Sam and Animal, but then Sam decided to go one way and Animal the other.

Sam twisted me around so that I had one arm in back of me leading him, and one arm in front, leading Animal. The gate was a distant hundred yards away. Kizzy looked on in amusement. I was a Push-Me-Pull-Me right out of Doctor Doolittle.

Weaving like a drunken sailor, I made my way over to the gate. Kizzy followed behind snorting, "Yo, ho, ho." Getting through the gate became the next problem. With halters held close, the three of us could not fit through. I threw an apple through the gate and hoped one of them would take the bait. Never one to miss a treat, Kizzy obliged and bolted past us. This created an impasse, because both Animal and Sam tried to fit through the gate at the same time with me in-between.

When it rains it pours. It started to rain. I landed splat on my face as Animal and Sam vaulted over me. It is a miracle I am still alive. Missing my head by a half an inch, the two nitwits galloped into the pasture not even bothering to look behind.

Later, I tried to explain the day's events to Ludwig and Pu. They were sorry for missing the horses' run for the border. After all, ordinarily you only see these things on television.

Truth is always stranger than fiction.

"But, Ludwig! The hooves missed me by a half an

inch!" I cried.

Ludwig gave me a hug and said, "Honey, we're glad you're all right. But, remember, adversity builds character."

"Character? Character? I have enough character! I don't WANT any more character!"

"Testing. Testing. Is anybody out there?" I continued, "I moved to the country for rest and relaxation, not survival training."

"Callie," Ludwig insisted, "You're just fine. Close only counts in horseshoes."

Easy for him to say. I looked up into the air and said, "I'd like to request a Guardian Angel, please."

Chapter Nine

Noah's Park

Ludwig, Pu, and I joined the Dog-of-the-Month Club. We figured one hundred and forty acres is a pretty big dog-run. We suffer from Alfalfa-on-the-Brain along with Canine Deficiency.

Each of us recalled unfulfilled childhood dreams. Pu had always longed for a Shetland Sheepdog, better known as a "Sheltie." I had always wanted one of those little wiener dogs. Ludwig had wanted a big dog. A really big dog, the biggest they make. So, if one person gets a brand-new dog, we all get a new dog, right? It's only fair.

We discovered "Oscar Wiener Dog" attempting to herd sheep at a nearby farm. A miniature Dachshund puppy is about as cute as they get. As I watched Oscar romp and play, he stole my heart and promised he'd be my baby forever, or at least stay small and cute.

Pu's Sheltie, "Cookie BaLu," came from the Animal Shelter. Cookie came to us with a broken leg, splint and all. Poor little Cookie hobbled valiantly, trying to keep up with the rest of the pups. Cookie's leg healed in due time, and she now herds horses and cattle. Constant barking, she believes, is the secret.

"Baby Bear" is the result of a mishap between two adjoining farms. A dairy farmer with two litters of puppies told us, "Here, take him. He's going to cost you a fortune to feed."

Baby Bear is a Newfoundland-German Shepherd cross, with the Newfoundland definitely outweighing the Shepherd. Full grown, Baby Bear weighs in at one-hundred forty pounds. Baby Bear told us he wanted a Rat Terrier puppy named "Jack-Sprat," and we foolishly obliged.

However, potty-training puppies is not my claim to fame. I assigned Sparky, the wonder dog, to this seemingly impossible task, and said, "Good luck. I'm putting you in charge." Sparky snapped the pups into formation and put them through rigorous basic training. Her success is downright Admirable.

While we were at it, I thought a couple of pygmy goats might fit right in with our farm picture. I bought Cleo and Zoe from the nuns in Middletown. Thinking goats would mow my lawn, I was chagrined when Cleo and Zoe got their signals crossed and ate the shrubs instead.

Instead of hiring a pesticide service, I purchased six cats from Mrs. Lindstrom, a.k.a. the Cat Lady. The Cat Lady is a widow of ten years, and Church Services daily delivers Meals on Wheels to her porch. No one has ever been inside Mrs. Lindstrom's house, and nobody wants to. Mrs. Lindstrom met me on her porch with a box full of cats, and said, "Here you go, dear. They're good mousers. They'll clear out your barn."

Upon the arrival of Mrs. Lindstrom's cats, the mice decided it was time to vacate the barn and made a mass exodus, Pied Piper style. I began to wonder what happened to all those brown perky eggs we didn't eat. I didn't give it a second thought, until I noticed an absence of chicken activity.

I own the laziest chickens in America. Why did the chicken cross the road? To get to Callie's for a free lunch. I walked into the barn and announced, "At least you could get up and take a walk once in awhile. What are you? Barn potatoes?" Finally, I actually saw a hen running around in the yard. "It's about time, lazy bones," I told her. She seemed pretty busy, and quickly darted back into the barn behind the alfalfa bales.

"Ok, what's going on in there?" I asked the bunch of them. "I know you're in there . . . somewhere."

I could see a row of chickens back behind the bales, sitting all lined up in a row. I thought it to be just about the oddest thing I've ever seen.

"Did you take a number for the deli?" I asked them. "Or are you in the return line?"

The Bantam hens did not budge an inch. They ignored me completely. Little Mel sat amongst the group. I looked at one of the Bantam roosters. I know he is a rooster because he has one of those big red floppy things on top of his head. I have two of them. Roosters, that is, not floppy red things on my head.

I asked Benny, the rooster, "Ok, what's up with these chicks? And how come the girls look so fat? It looks like they've quadrupled in size."

Benny did not answer, so I tried to budge one of the hens. The hen went into attack mode. "Oh, boy," I said aloud, "What's the deal here?"

I went to the house and returned, wearing leather gloves. Elmer and Wilbur wanted to know why I was disturbing their nap time. (Nap time for Elmer and Wilbur is twenty-four hours a day, seven days a week.)

"Okay, move it boys," I told them. "I have to get back behind you."

"Esther, honey, I have to move you over to see what is going on here," I said to the black-feathered hen. Esther hissed at me. "Oh, so that's how you're going to be . . . " Just then I saw movement underneath Esther. "What in the world?"

To my amazement, little round fluffy golf balls scurried out from beneath Esther and scattered this way and that. I stood with my mouth wide open.

"Oh, my word . . . this is like a miracle or something," I said aloud. I felt like I had just given birth. I felt awed to witness such creation. I tried to count the chicks as they scampered out from under. Fourteen! I think.

"Oh, Esther, will you let me hold one?" I asked her.

Multicolored chicks scooted beneath my feet. Esther ran, dashing to and fro, attempting to keep her babies in a group. I picked up one of the chicks, and Esther apparently decided a round-up was more important.

I looked up into the air and laughed, "Do you know how cool this is? I can't believe it. Thank you!"

The air did not answer back, but there was a warm breeze that day. I could swear I heard, "Glad you like it! It tickles my heart too!"

Esther decided she'd do her own tickling, and bit my leg. "Ok, Esther, here you go," I said handing over her baby.

How in the world she missed one baby out of fourteen I do not know. Two days later Esther decided the youngins' were ready for World Studies 101. She proudly strutted out of the barn with fourteen children by her side. Mother Esther's task for the day, and every day thereafter, was to teach her babies how to scratch and peck.

Esther scratches the ground, pulls the grass apart, and looks to see what is underneath. All fourteen chicks look and peck where she scratches, and Esther picks up little pieces of something or other and lets them know they should probably eat this. When the chicks satisfy Esther with their looking and pecking, Esther rushes over to a new untried spot.

Of course, Elmer and Wilbur think this to be great fun, being the resident sod layers. They want to know exactly what Esther is looking for, because they want some of it, too. Esther pecks at the dirt, and Elmer and Wilbur search for invisible food.

Esther's cohorts also vacated the barn, and lo and behold, that martial row of hens marched out with an entire army by their side. My perky brown eggs did, indeed, have baby chicks inside. They hatched into a sea of fluff.

Each hen had been sitting on at least fifteen eggs, including Little Mel. Little Mel didn't care whether or not she sat on her own eggs, she just figured, "If I sat on them, they're mine. What's due is due." With eight hens hatching approximately twelve chicks each, this brought the grand total to over one-hundred chickens!

Stanley, the peacock, oversaw poultry production. His tail grew back in all its splendor, and he became the Flutter Master of Alfalfabit Soup. Spreading his tail, Stanley busily fanned it in front of the poultry orchestra, moving them this way and that, conducting them in all his multicolored glory.

Cleo and Zoe, the goats, indicated their approval of the maternity ward by bouncing in and out of flocks of chicks, running and leaping into mid air, to and fro.

The four new puppies stuck their noses into the hustle and bustle. My ignorance is bliss. I thought, "If I can just teach them to all get along . . . "

Esther and the other hens resolved the problem by simply scaring the daylights out of the puppies. The pups learned the true meaning of being "henpecked." Puppies yelped, looked frantically for Mom, and ran with tails between their legs.

"Now see?" I told the pups, "You leave those chicks alone. Everybody has to get along around here."

I adopted a "sink or swim" motto. Calling all of them together, I stood on the back stoop, addressing the citizens of my new kingdom. I wondered if this is how Noah felt.

"Now listen up, everybody," I said to one-hundred and six chickens, five dogs, six cats, two pigs, two goats, three horses, four cows, and a peacock in a pear tree, "I have called you all together for an important message. Freedom is the issue. Freedom is yours, if you wish to partake in this program. This could mean life or death. I hope you will choose life. The lion WILL lay down with the lamb. Get it?"

"Thy will be done," I added. And I truly believed it COULD be.

• • •

Ludwig, Pu, and I sat at the kitchen table, looking out the window into the cow pasture. Flower, Margie, and Henrietta were due to give birth any minute. Our neighbor, Earl, had told us, "You really don't have to do anything for calving. The cows will do the work, you just have to keep an eye on them. They'll 'drop' them in the pasture."

"What's that black dog doing in the middle of the pasture?" Ludwig asked.

"What black dog?" asked Pu and I.

"I think a black dog is after the cows!" exclaimed Ludwig.

"Well, what are we going to do, Ludwig?" I asked.

"I'll go out and chase him away," he responded.

Pu and I flew out the door after Ludwig in case our services were needed. Getting to the middle of the pasture is quite a hike, and we found it unusual that the "black dog" was not running around like a maniac chasing cows. In fact, the black dog had apparently lain down in the grass for a snooze.

Henrietta didn't care about the black dog. What she cared about was our walking toward her. Marty grazed a short distance away from Henrietta. We all started to laugh.

"Why, that's not a dog! It's a calf!" we exclaimed.

Henrietta knew darn well it was a calf and pawed the ground, hunched herself down, and glared at us with a wild eyed, I've-lost-my-mind kind of look. I call it the, "I'm going to kill you," look. The black Angus bull was not our immediate concern, Henrietta was.

"Everybody out!" ordered Ludwig.

Henrietta didn't come at us straight on--she lunged left and right in a zig-zag charge. Our screams did not help matters.

"Run!" yelled Ludwig.

Decisions, decisions. Henrietta was forced to decide whether to kill us or stay with her calf. She chose the former. Seconds count when you're running for your life.

"Run Pu!" I hollered. "Run for the fence!"

Ludwig stayed a few steps behind Pu and me, willing to put his life on the line. "Just keep going," he yelled. "Don't look back! Don't look back, whatever you do!"

Not wanting to be turned into pillars of salt like Lot's wife, Pu and I fled Henrietta's sulfuric wrath. We did not look back, however tempting. Henrietta stopped short of trampling Ludwig. Pu and I made the fence-line.

"Hurry, Dad!" Pu yelled.

Henrietta, thankfully, chose that moment to look back at her calf. She swung her head at us, snorted, turned around, and ambled back to her baby.

The three of us leaned on the fence, huffing and puffing.

"It's a good thing she didn't turn you into a cow pie," I told Ludwig.

"I would have been a pie in the sky," he laughed.

• • •

Marty, Flower, Margie, Henrietta and her new calf, Bulls Eye, scampered about the pasture. The five of them played an in-and-out game, coming and going from the cattle shed. The cattle shed has a smaller, fenced area which opens onto the big pasture.

After our death-defying escape, I called Larry and Del, the Norwegian bachelor farmers, to see if our cows are insane. I couldn't forget the look in Henrietta's eyes.

"No," Larry laughed, "but you never vant to get bettveen a calf and the modder!"

I can attest to this fact. Too bad sometimes I don't read my own writing. Or, perhaps, the clear writing on the wall.

I sat at the kitchen table, sipping coffee, while Pu and Ludwig prepared to go their respective ways.

"Callie, can you check on the cows this morning?" Ludwig asked.

"Sure, as long as I don't have to go inside the pen," I answered.

"Oh, they'd never hurt you," replied Ludwig.

I hesitated, wondering if this would be one of those days. "All right, I'll check on them," I answered.

I made my way down to the cattle shed, waving cheerful goodbyes to Pu and Ludwig. "Have a good day!" I yelled to them. "Love you!"

"Love you, too!" they answered back.

In the fenced paddock area, Henrietta busied herself with Bulls Eye. Flower looked on wistfully, obviously wanting a calf of her own. Marty stood outside the shed door looking very doormanly. I assumed Margie was inside the shed. Though the cattle shed is open to the fenced area, I couldn't see inside. I heard moaning. Marty looked at me, expecting me to do something.

"Uh oh," I said aloud.

I decided I needed to move the cows out of the smaller paddock and into the pasture in order to assess the situation. I ran to the big barn and returned with a bag of corn. I spread it out on the pasture ground, outside the fenced paddock. Marty, Flower, Henrietta, and Bulls Eye dashed through the open gate, and I locked it behind them.

The moaning continued.

"Margie, is that you?" I asked, dreading the answer.

My eyes adjusted to the dimness inside the cattle shed. Margie lay on her side, crying wail after wail.

"Oh, great!" I sighed. So much for "dropping" them in the pasture.

The problem, as I saw it, was that I couldn't very well run back to the house, call a vet and expect him to get here in time. Margie lay there with a calf's head sticking out of her. Amazed at the size of the head, I could hardly ignore the placenta still covering the calf's head.

Constance recently told me about a foal she had lost because it never punctured the embryonic sack during the birthing process. The foal drowned in the fluid. Not knowing how long the calf's head had been sticking out of Margie, I felt helpless. Margie looked at me, pleadingly.

The calf did not move, but then, I really didn't know if it should. Its front legs were still inside. Margie lifted her head off the ground and moaned again.

Breathing appeared to me to be the priority. The calf needed to breathe.

I hesitated, but then summoned my courage. I walked up behind Margie, hoping she would accept my presence. Did this come under the category of getting between a calf and its "modder?" No matter. I had to take the chance.

I didn't know how to puncture the embryonic sack, and the house was too far away. I searched the ground for a stick. I punctured the sack with the stick, not knowing what outcome to expect. I gently pulled the sack away from the calf's face, anticipating its taking a breath. The calf did not breathe.

I stood back, and stared at Margie. How long could she lie there with a dead calf sticking out of her? Margie looked exhausted. Kneeling behind Margie, I put my mouth over the calf's nose, and cupped my hands around its face. I blew softly into the calf's nostrils. Hopefully, CPR is CPR.

On the fifth try, the most amazing big, brown eyes blinked back at me.

"Oh, my word!" I exclaimed.

Margie lifted her head, anxious to know what was going on back there.

"Come on, Margie," I told her. "Please? You can do it!"

"No, I can't," she seemed to reply, putting her head back down on the ground spent. She moaned again.

"Oh, Lord, how am I going to do this?" I asked aloud. "How am I supposed to deliver this calf?"

I remembered the Scripture verse, "Everything is possible for him who believes." This certainly came under the "everything" category.

Tears ran down my face.

"Okay," I said, wiping the sweat off my brow, "I'll

give it a try."

I reached up inside of Margie to try to feel for the calf's legs. They were bent, not in the proper "dive" position, as I later learned. The calf was definitely stuck.

"Okay, Margie," I told her, "all I can do is pull, but I'll sure pull!"

Margie moaned her response.

The situation was bizarre. The calf's head was sticking out. It was breathing, looking around, but it couldn't get out!

"Oh, Margie, I hope I don't break you in two!" I cried.

I took hold of the calf's head, and put my feet on either side of Margie's back end. I tugged, and tugged and tugged. I increased the intensity with each pull.

Finally . . . the calf's shoulders squeezed through. With the shoulders out, the front legs slipped out from behind. I later learned that sometimes farmers have to use a chain and a pickup truck in order to pull the calf out.

It looked as if the calf was going to get up and walk around, but he was still missing his back half. I moved away from the calf and confronted Margie.

"I sure hope you can finish the job, Margie!"

I gave her a few minutes. Margie regained some strength and began to push. The calf's back legs emerged.

"That a girl!" I told her.

The calf lay there for a few minutes, and then struggled for an upright position. Margie, herself, rose to the occasion.

"Well, I don't know what to do next, Margie. I sure hope you do," I told her.

"We'll be fine, now," she seemed to say, focusing all of her attention on the newborn. Margie decided her calf needed a good toweling off, and she began her motherly chore, glancing at me.

"Thank you so very much," I saw in her eyes, "But you may go now and leave us alone."

I named our new calf, "Pizza Pie." I called Ludwig at the office and interrupted his truck dispatching.

"Ludwig!" I cried. "We now have pizza delivery on the farm! I delivered a pizza!"

"Pepperoni?" he asked.

"No, beef!" I replied.

Chapter Ten

Machinery Hill

Put a Swede saw in the hands of a Swede and you'll see some action. I don't know the history of this useful tool, I only know that, if it breaks, we must have another one before the sun sets.

Ludwig was not born to be wild. He was born to prune trees. It has been duly noted that men and women do not see eye to eye on how a tree should look.

"Let them just grow," is my motto. I cannot get past the, "It will grow better if it is pruned," approach.

Take a Swede saw out of the hands of a Swede and replace it with a chainsaw, and you will experience a main event versus a warm up. The Swede Saw Massacre.

Thank goodness we were blessed with an entire woods scattered with dead trees. Not anymore. It was a call to arms and another Swede arrived for active duty with his Swede saw. However, being Norwegian myself, I must say that it was only when a hefty Norwegian showed up that the big trees began to fall.

The Swedes stood back with Swede saws in hand and watched in awe as the mighty Norwegian wielded a mean axe, chain saw, and a forceful push. Tiiimmmbbbeeerrrr!

I only bring nationalities into this scenario because for years Ludwig has told me, "The Swedes taught the Norwegians how to climb down from the trees."

Forget the Swede saw; if a Swede is up in a tree, bring a hefty Norwegian with an axe to grind. He'll teach him how to get down from a tree.

The two Swedes and the Norwegian stood back from their handiwork lovingly surveying a pile of brush the size of a two story building.

"That's some pile," I said. "Are there any trees left?"

The two Swedes and the Norwegian eagerly responded, "Yah, sure, you bettcha. The other trees need room to grow."

I was afraid to ask, "What are you going to do with the pile?"

How premature of me. Ludwig pulled out a blowtorch the size of a small cannon. And thus, my first brush pile experience ignited. It was the first of many.

"You can't burn that," I told him.

"Of course I can," replied Ludwig. "It's a brush pile. We're in the country. I have a permit."

"Ludwig, you need a fire truck standing by. You'll set the whole county ablaze."

Ludwig pointed to the Norwegian. "He's done this lots of times."

I looked at my pyromaniac in disbelief. "If you think I'm going to stand around and watch you incinerate the county . . ." I said.

"We'll dig ditches if the fire spreads, but it's not going to. This is a contained fire. Just watch . . ."

Ludwig lit the torch and the dead wood caught fire instantaneously. The four of us bolted back from the blaze of heat.

"Wow! Look at her go!" the men cried.

The flames shot up into the sky, and black smoke billowed up into the air. I stood back, waiting for the sound of sirens. Two-hundred black crows flew over our heads, vacating the premises.

"Won't people report us, Ludwig?" I asked.

"Nah . . . everybody does this out here. Isn't it great?"

"Anybody want some hotdogs?" asked the Norwegian, as he pulled out wieners and buns from his pickup.

"I brought the sodas," said the Swede.

• • •

Thank goodness, it was Wednesday. Every Wednesday is Ladies League at the bowling alley. At eleven o'clock we always gather for lunch at the Plugged Artery and muster our spirits before "bowling up a storm," as Peg puts it. Of course, Peg can talk; she's the only one who ever hits a 170.

"I'm so mad I can't see straight," she announced.

Pre-bowling lunch is when we ladies let off our steam. Peg's face looked like her heart was going to blow.

"That Charlie, if he cuts down one more tree!"

We all looked at each other and realized we all had the same problem.

"How many chain saws do you have?" I asked Peg.

"Four, counting the one Grandma gave me. Charlie has five, in case one quits."

Constance piped up, "We have seven, and that's not counting the Swede saws."

"That Charlie went and cut down all the trees we planted twenty years ago," Peg wept into her iced tea.

"That's nothing," said Constance, "Our backyard keeps moving back two-hundred feet a year. I'm mowing five acres and soon it's going to be ten."

Quiet little Meg whispered, "We have a chain saw collection. Bill has been collecting them ever since I met him in high school. He brings them out and shows them to company."

"That is a tough one, Meg," I sympathized. "How many do you figure you have?"

"Thirty-six," she sighed.

"Whoa!" we all gasped.

"What is it with these men and their saws?" I wanted to know. "Has this been going on throughout the centuries?" I thought perhaps it was time to analyze this addiction. "What if we were to take away their saws, do you think they'd go into withdrawl?"

"Oh, yeah, without a doubt," replied Constance, the saw-addiction director, "You'd have to take them away slowly. And I mean slowly, one saw at a time."

"Twelve-step saw reduction?" I asked.

"But then, if you did that, you'd have to work on the driveway dilemma too," added Constance.

"Driveway dilemma?" I was confused.

"You mean to say he hasn't hit you up for a new driveway yet?" asked Constance.

"No," I replied.

"Just wait," she answered, ominously.

• • •

Living in the country can bring out the oddest contra-

dictions in a marriage. Women prefer their country driveways with a little grass strip running down the middle.
We think it's cute.

In all our years of marriage I had never really seen
Ludwig behind the wheel of a huge semi, tractor-trailer.
I was playing with Elmer and Wilbur out by the drive-
way when I saw a semi careening down our driveway.

"Oh, my word!" I cried.

To my surprise, Ludwig's face was behind the wheel.
The huge truck reminded me of an apartment building
on wheels. My first thought was, "Does he even know
how to drive that thing?"

Ludwig burped the brakes into a jolting stop. Elmer
and Wilbur scattered into the wind.

"Hi, honey, I'm home," he said.

"Ludwig, you come down out of there before you get
hurt!" I cried.

"Callie, Callie, Callie," he said, "I do this for a living."

"I thought you just dispatched trucks. Are you sure
you know how to drive one of those things? How are
you going to turn it around? And why on earth is it
here?"

"I'm going to fix the driveway," he responded.

"Uh oh, the 'driveway'," I whispered to myself.

"I have a load of gravel in the back."

Now I understood only too well why Ludwig had
bought all that machinery from the previous farmer.
Ludwig stored his graders, harrows, brush-hog and blades
behind the barn.

The little ruts in the driveway soon gave way to truck-
loads of class-five roadway material. Ludwig gleefully

plowed up the little grass strip in the name of progress.

I took Ludwig a soda and asked, "Are you sure you know how to do all of this?"

He replied, "I used to build air strips in the Moroccan desert."

"Yes. That would make sense. Is there anything else I don't know about you?"

I didn't know that Ludwig's tractor would soon become a very dear friend. A man driving a tractor is like a kid hitting a home run at his first Little League game. Our driveway was soon smooth and wide and resembled nothing so much as a municipal airstrip.

When all was said and done, Ludwig, Pu and I sat in the front porch swing admiring the skyline. The electric bug light sputtered and crackled.

"The bug light is just like the Fourth-of-July," commented Ludwig.

"Why, yes it is! It's amazing what we find amusing, isn't it?" I laughed.

Pu remarked, "It sure is." She looked at us as if we were from another planet.

Just then we heard engines up in the sky. A small plane came into view, and we all stood up in astonishment.

"Do you think he's in trouble?" I asked Ludwig.

The engines began to sputter and crackle. The engines suddenly went dead.

"Oh no!" I cried.

"Don't worry," replied Ludwig, "He's got our driveway in sight."

"Yep," I said. "He's coming in for a landing all right."

Silence grew around us as we waited for the inevi-
table. The wheels came down, the pilot waggled the
plane a bit, and brought it in within fifty-feet of the front
porch.

"Now, see?" Ludwig told me, "You just never know,
Callie."

"No. You never do know, do you? You made a very
nice runway, Ludwig. I'm very proud of you."

"Way to go, Dad," said Pu.

Chapter Eleven

Birds of a Feather

The large, smooth, warm egg felt soothing to my ear. I listened carefully for signs of life. "Peep, peep, peep," I whispered. I am probably the only person in America walking around with a peacock egg held to her ear. I highly recommend it.

Stanley had needed a likeness. While he appeared quite content to run with the hens and play traffic director, I felt sorry for him. Peacocks are not easy to locate.

Persistence usually pays off in the end, however, and I am the mistress of persistence. Just ask Ludwig or Pu. They say it's very hard to get me to let go of the bone, let alone allow them to throw it. Just a figure of speech.

If it's out there, I'll find it. If there is a will, there is a way, but it might have to be Callie's Way. This persistence, which sometimes rears its head as stubbornness, comes from Viking horns, I believe. There seems to be no other explanation as to why someone would wear a bowl with horns on her head, if not for stubbornness. It's simply in my genes.

• • •

One-hundred year-old Grandma Erickson sat in her chair one day, blinked at me in shock, and asked, "Vere does DIS come from?" in response to my recital of my latest life events on running a farm.

"This, WHAT, Grandma?" I replied, frantically trying to understand what she meant.

"Dis . . . dis . . . " she stuttered trying to find the word, "dis . . . "

"My craziness?" I asked, helpfully.

"No, no, no!" she answered back, defiantly. "Dis DRIVE! You're so driven!"

I looked back at her in shocked recognition. We sat there together, eating our peppermints, a mirror image of one another, with age our only separation. I burst out laughing.

"Why . . . I think it comes from YOU!"

Her eyes grew as wide as a piece of lefse.

"Grandma, may I remind you. You were the one who came over alone on the boat from Norway at sixteen. And you think I am driven? You probably drove the boat."

She chuckled, slapping her knee a little bit, with the most gorgeous twinkles shining in her bright blue eyes. "Punker," she said softly, "You'll always be my Punker."

"Grandma, I like to refer to this drive as strength. I get my strength from you."

We hugged, as we always do, and she felt bad that she couldn't offer me a slice of brown goat cheese. Grandma went home to be with the Lord that year, but I'll be her little Punker forever.

• • •

I located "The Bird Man" in a little town called Isle Corner, thirty miles due west. Otto Kirkegaard had been studying birds for over fifty years and had quite a collection in his back yard. Otto allowed me to pick from his female peahens, and I went home with two lovely girls named Audrey and Carmen.

It amazes me how an animal can recognize its own. Stanley immediately abandoned the chickens and took up with Audrey and Carmen in the corn crib. The girls weren't all that excited about allowing Stanley to be their traffic director, but gave way in due time. If Grandma thought I was driven, she'd have gotten a kick out of Stanley. Stanley does a Viking proud.

Stanley rustles his tail for a pre-announcement of sorts, and then flutters it into full bloom. In full bloom, Stanley takes a stance and stiffens his body so that he will be able to support what is over a five-foot tail-spread. He reminds me of Lucy Ricardo in a rumba number. Or, Lucy in a Viking hat.

Stanley cannot move very quickly in full tail-spread. He waddles in short, stiff, staccato steps. While stepping staunchly to whatever music must be running in his head, he whistles his wings while he walks.

Audrey and Carmen took their residency in the corn crib quite seriously. They became housebound, and I began to worry. Donning leather gloves once again, I approached the girls and tried to loft them off their fat behinds. My little brown Bantam eggs dwarfed in comparison to what I discovered. Seven peacock eggs.

Audrey and Carmen sat on their eggs for a couple of days and then left town like a couple of disgruntled hussies. Peahens have little foo-foo's sticking out of their heads like feathered, showgirl headresses. Audrey and

Carmen would fit right into the Vegas scene, with Stanley as the Master of Ceremonies.

I called Otto, the Bird Man.

"Otto! I don't know what's wrong with these girls! They're not sitting on their eggs, and it looks like they have no intention of doing so. They have no motherly instincts at all!"

"Yah . . . " he answered slowly. I could practically see Otto scratching his head under his Carhartt hat. "Those birds are a strange bunch. They're kinda stupid. Sometimes they forget they've laid eggs. You might have to incubate them."

"Incubate? How do I incubate?"

"Yah, you have to find an incubator. It won't be easy to find one for peacock eggs. Tell you what I'll do. I'll lend you mine."

The showgirls did not miss their seven eggs and spent every waking moment rehearsing dance numbers with Stanley. Pu and I were in charge of incubation. We followed the instructions, but I became extremely worried that I might actually be cooking the peacocks inside the eggs. The very thought made my skin crawl. Hard-boiled peacocks.

Incubation time neared its close. I checked on the eggs hourly, sometimes minutely. The incubator sat on the kitchen counter next to the flour and sugar canisters. At dinnertime, the three of us heard strange noises coming from inside the incubator.

"Oh, my!" I cried.

The sounds were very muffled. Each of us picked up an egg and put it to our ears. The eggs were warm from the incubator and felt soothing against our ears.

"Peep, peep, peep," they said.

"Peep, peep, peep," we answered back.

We walked around with eggs coming out of our ears, trying to be very careful not to jostle them. We cooed and peeped for hours on end. We ate dinner with eggs in our ears. We watched TV with eggs in our ears. Pu invited friends over to put eggs in their ears.

Finally, to our absolute delight, we noticed a very small hole in one of the eggs with a tiny point of a beak sticking through. We were thrilled!

"Should we help them out?" I asked.

"No, we need to let them come out on their own," Ludwig decided.

"But it's so tempting, Ludwig!"

Five eggs hatched.

Five baby peacocks lived in a plastic tub in the living room for weeks. They imprinted to us from birth, thinking we were peacocks, or they humans, we do not know which. Just as I had trained my baby squirrels from years ago, I helped the peacocks to the outside world. The only difference? I didn't sit in a tree, I became the tree.

The babies perched on my shoulders, and we went on with our business of doing chores together. I talked to them, and they answered me back. We had many a lively conversation. I call this form of communication "blurping."

This is how to talk baby peacock: Make a high-pitched sound in the throat. Create bursting, bubbly sounds through lips. It is not highly attractive, but then blurping rarely is.

After about three months, each bird grew to the size of a small turkey. Perched on my shoulders, they made my shoulders begin to sag, until I resembled an old woman with osteoporosis. The peacocks played King of the Hill, and I was the hill.

Lucky, Levi, Louise, Lois, and Loretta dive-bombed me from treetop heights and forced me to wear suitable armor for the carrier landings. Of course, they couldn't all fit on my shoulders anymore, and this signified a constant fight for territory.

It became impossible to keep the Quints in the house any longer. They knew the exact location of the refrigerator and where I keep the tomato soup. Weaning them with tomato soup was probably a dumb move on my part, because our prize tomato plants disappeared just in time for the County Fair.

And so, over the summer, the birds spread out through the farm, each finding a special spot to nest depending on the time of day. Animals follow the sun. Lucky follows the pickup truck. Lucky has taken over ownership of the pickup truck, and we are not supposed to drive it. Lucky lives in the box of the pickup.

To our dismay, Ludwig took off one day for the hardware store without checking the back of the truck. Lucky ended up in Waterdale and ate lunch with Ludwig at the Plugged Artery. Susan, the waitress, served Lucky a grilled cheese sandwich and a cup of tomato soup. Ludwig left a big tip. So did Lucky.

It is true that peacocks make good watch dogs. They scream, "Help," at any unsuspecting farm visitor, and we began receiving calls from neighbors wanting to know if we were still alive.

"We hear screams for help coming from your farm," they informed us. "Are you sure you're all right?"

We were . . . for the moment.

• • •

Ludwig and I were asleep upstairs in the bedroom. Well before dawn, I awoke in the pitch dark for some reason, with panic rising in my throat. Mothers have an ability to sense any type of movement while in deep sleep. Our DNA makes us "motion detectors."

Ludwig did not stir because he is not equipped with a motion detector. I got out of bed, quiet as a mouse, and tiptoed through the upstairs. I am the hall monitor.

I did not put on the light for fear of revealing my whereabouts to a potential intruder. Just outside the bathroom doorway, I took one step onto the soft carpet. My heart stopped beating. I felt a painful pinch on my big toe, like someone giving it an injection. Only, the needle of the "injection" actually moved. Muffled by darkness I was paralyzed by terror. I could not scream. I wanted to faint.

My big toe detected not only a needle-like object, but something soft, like hair.

"I think I'm going to die," my brain told me. My mind went on the fritz, unable to compute a connection between needles and hair.

The hairy-needle thing stuck to my toe, and I struggled to walk to a light switch. I dragged the hairy-needle behind me, half expecting a boa constrictor or a rabid bat to finish me off. I pinched myself, hoping it was a nightmare. No nightmare, this is my life.

I reached the light switch. Better off not knowing. A hairy mouse had sunk his teeth into my big toe and was stuck to it. Ludwig, wake up! Your wife is dying, and you're going to miss it!

I attempted speech, but it had deserted me. I waved my extremities, frantically hoping Ludwig might telepathically come to my aid. I kicked my leg up into the air several times, shaking my foot like a spastic chorus girl. The mouse let go and went flying five feet across the length of the hallway to land splat against the wall.

The mouse hit the wall at high velocity some four feet up in the air, bounced off, and landed below on the carpet. I thought I had killed him. He lay there for a moment.

I had only stunned him. Swaggering like a convict on the run, he felt his way along the baseboard, inching his way toward the doorway to the spare bedroom. I reached out to catch him, but caught myself from doing so. Pick up a live mouse? I don't think so.

Timing was the key. I needed to locate some kind of object to contain him before he disappeared into a closet, never to be seen again. I ran to the closet door and said, "Oh, no, you don't." He changed directions and headed for the next wall. I ran downstairs, tore the cupboards apart and hightailed it back upstairs with an empty ice cream bucket. I placed the upside down bucket on top of him, and added a heavy dictionary on top of that.

Exhausted, I returned to the side of my sleeping

Ludwig. I growled softly at Prince Charming, and he reached over and patted me with closed eyes and said, "That's nice, dear . . . "

I slipped inside the sheets just in time to notice a shadow going across the window from right to left behind the mini-blinds. Obviously, my motion detector had been operating correctly. I now had two nightmares for the price of one.

The shadow returned, this time moving from left to right.

"Shotgun," I whispered to Ludwig. "Shotgun. Where is the shotgun?"

"Hmmm? Hmmm?" he muttered.

"WAKE UP, Ludwig," I entreated him.

The shadow returned, right to left. It suddenly bobbed up and down.

"Ouch!" squealed Ludwig.

"Get up and protect me!" I hissed, while pinching him sharply.

"From what?" he asked, sitting up and yawning.

"There's someone outside the window," I whispered.

"Should I call the police?" he said, suddenly sort of wide awake.

"They won't have time to get here. We'll be dead."

Ludwig got out of bed and went to the closet. He returned with the shotgun, and we sat up wide awake, staring at the window. The only problem was, we couldn't remember where we put the shotgun shells.

"Callie," he said reasonably. "We're on the second floor. Why would someone be walking by the window on the second floor? The roof is slanted."

"I don't know, who knows how they plan these things?" I whispered. "Who knows what their twisted minds have concocted?"

"I haven't seen anything. Where did they go?" Ludwig inquired.

"Shhh!" I insisted. "There. There it is! The shadow!"

The shadow stopped. The shadow stopped right in front of the window. We dimly made out a hunched shape through the mini-blinds.

"We're dead," I whispered. "They heard us. Now they know we're awake. They'll have to kill us instead of just robbing the place. We're out in the middle of nowhere."

The shadow knocked on the window. Tap. Tap. Tap. I clung to Ludwig.

"I don't want to die. Not like this!" I cried into his shoulder. "I'm so glad Pu's at a friend's house. They probably staked us out. They have fewer people to kill this way."

Tap. Tap. Tap.

We sat in silence. Waiting. Waiting for the sound of breaking glass.

Tap. Tap. Tap.

"It sounds like they want to come in," Ludwig whispered.

"Like they're asking for permission."

"Well, by all means, ask them in for a midnight snack," I cringed.

"I'm going to open it," Ludwig replied, getting up to open the window.

"I can't look," I whimpered.

Ludwig flung open the mini-blinds. The mini-blinds rattled and crashed to the floor. Ludwig screamed, "I've got a shotgun!"

The shadow screamed, "Help!"

Ludwig stood confronting a terrified Lucky. Lucky continued to scream for "Help!"

"Lucky!" I cried. "Lucky, it's you!"

"Lucky, is right!" Ludwig returned. "He's downright lucky I don't have shells in this shotgun."

Lucky stopped screaming.

Tap. Tap. Tap.

"Ah . . . he wants to come in," I said, lovingly.

"Please let me come in. It's cold outside," Lucky seemed to say. "How about a cup of tomato soup?"

Ludwig cupped the shotgun trigger, and said, "You're lucky to be alive! I'm going back to bed!"

"Yes, Ludwig, come back to bed. I've had enough excitement for one night."

Just then, I thought of the mouse in the house trapped under the ice cream bucket. "Just a minute," I said. "I'll be right back."

Certainly, my eyes deceived me. My mouse was running laps around the bottom of the ice cream bucket at top speed. His laps became so fast that he began to climb the bucket just like one of those motorcycles at a circus that finally ends up flying upside down. Varoom!

"I guess it's your lucky night, too, mouse. Better try to get some sleep. Tomorrow you may get to join the circus."

Chapter Twelve

Angels Have Heard on High

"It's a three-ring circus around here!" I told Ludwig and Pu. "Rural life is supposed to be quiet. Uneventful."

I took a deep breath. Breathing deeply too soon, I tried to gag a scream. I was simply trying to put bread into the toaster.

PuLaRoo ran over to see what was the matter, and then sprinted the other way. A mouse peered back from the toaster slot and then slipped down into the toaster springs. I grabbed a magazine, slammed it on the top of the toaster, and said, "Somebody open the back door."

"There's always more than one mouse in the house," Ludwig remarked, casually.

I groaned and walked the toaster out to the back stoop and dumped the contents over the railing. Elmer and Wilbur squealed, adding to the mayhem. Wilbur was hogging the mud puddle again. I had shoveled out a three-foot by two-foot hole in the ground and filled it with a foot of water. Elmer and Wilbur troweled and scooped the sides of the hole, creating just the right consistency for slime mud. Slime mud is different from regular mud in that a pig will practically knead it like a loaf of bread. The most hilarious aspect of the slime mud production was watching the two of them blow bubbles in the water.

Elmer and Wilbur apply this slime mud as a protective coating over their skin. Looking like they just had facials at a spa, they emerged fully protected from sunburn or biting insects.

"Well, I wouldn't exactly call it quiet with Elmer and Wilbur on the premises," Ludwig said, in a relaxed tone.

Always one for reflection, I reminisced over our lifestyle change.

"Do you think we made the right choice, Ludwig?" I asked.

"I mean, sometimes it seems like it's too much. Like I can't keep up. Things keep happening. Every time I turn around, I run into another surprise."

"Would you rather have an uneventful life, Callie? Would you really?" asked Ludwig.

I thought for a moment.

"It has been a wild ride, hasn't it?" I slowly grinned at Ludwig. "Who would have thought?"

The three of us sat at the kitchen table. A new day dawned. The sun erased doubts.

"Sometimes I am just amazed. Can you believe how much we've learned out here?" I asked the two of them. "How much we've learned about ourselves? As a family?"

We'd developed into a team. Worked as a unit. Fought the odds. Struggled. Laughed. Cried.

Our lifestyle change was a risk, to be sure. Venturing into the unknown is not comfortable by any means. But, what an adventure. What a ride!

Mrs. Organization learned how to put her preconceived notions aside. Daily routines became nonexistent, because that is what happens on a farm. Stuff happens.

It became a surrendering of self, in a way. Acceptance in knowing we are not alone. Too much had occurred to deny it. My journey into the unknown had matured into a mission of faith.

• • •

"What? You're assigning me to Callie Carlson again? I'd like to put in for an immediate transfer, please," announced Guardian Angel, first-class, Stonebrook.

Stonebrook huddled with angels Alfonse and Fulton, unable to believe his misfortune. Fulton clasped the marching orders in his left hand and held a thick file, Volume Five, under his right arm.

"I'm afraid the orders are not to be denied," Fulton concluded.

Stonebrook attempted to explain the upcoming mission to Fulton.

"Do you know how hard it is to keep that girl alive? I mean, come on. We need a team, Fulton! It's too big a job for one angel!"

Alfonse nodded in agreement. "It took two of us to stop that exercise bicycle. Remember when she got her hand stuck in the spokes? It took all of our strength to stop the spinning before her hand snapped in two. We couldn't allow hand-amputation because it wasn't in her plan."

"I agree completely," said Fulton, "She's no easy assignment. But, Stonebrook, you're up. Beatrice is begging for a replacement. Our subject has moved out to a farm, and Beatrice's allergies maxed out. Pack some ear plugs, because she says the pig squealing will rupture your eardrums."

"I suppose Beatrice gets Broadway?" Stonebrook asked sarcastically. "What's this place called? 'Alfalfabit Soup?'"

Stonebrook shuffled his feet in the cloud dust and toed SOS in the soft white crystals. Alfonse touched his arm consolingly and said, "Don't worry, I'll help you. Skylar and his team have the next door neighbor's house, and Beatrice will still be around. The entire region is covered, per usual.

"You'll have all the help you need," Fulton reassured them. "All you have to do is ask."

• • •

Ludwig and Pu hurried out the door for work and school. Later that morning, thunderous clouds moved in and I watched as a massive storm approached. Standing on the front wraparound porch, I winced as lightning cracked across what seemed to be hundreds of miles of sky. I estimated the storm's arrival time to be forty-five minutes. The horses had already been put out for the day and needed to be stalled before the storm hit.

I observed Animal, Sam, and Kizzy unhappily piled up at the gate. Horses do not like storms. Horses like warm, safe, dry stalls.

Animals have two defenses––fight or flight. A horse's mind is calibrated for flight. Horses do not think when they are in a frenzy.

"Oh, you guys have plenty of time before it hits," I

told them. "You'll all be snug in your beds before the raindrops fall."

I grabbed a halter off the nail sticking out of the fence board. The horses shuffled for position. They maneuvered frantically for the front gate position, while pointing their heads in my direction for halter attachment. They wanted out, and bad.

I reached over the metal-rung gate and haltered Kizzy. Just as I was pulling her out of the line of fire through the half-open gate, I saw Sam's back end come up.

In slow motion, I noticed the rippled effect of his hind quarter muscles. Both back legs came up off the ground and bent as he targeted his hooves on Kizzy. He missed.

My eyes zeroed in on the two hooves rocketing toward me and contact. A split second can carry with it a myriad of movement. At the same time, my hand reached down to try to lock the gate, realizing the other two horses would barrel through. One hoof blasted the gatepost, the other, the gate itself.

Attempting to lock the gate aligned my face with the top rung of the metal. When Sam snapped the gatepost half out of the ground, it added extra force to the gate collision. As the metal gate cracked against my face, I was thrown backwards, reeling midair. At the same time, my hand closed over the lead-rope attached to Kizzy's halter. My mind tried to connect with my hand, and said, "Hold onto the horse," which was actually a very foolish thing to do. It is better to loose a riled horse if one has no control.

At impact, my mind raced ahead of itself. "This is a

bad one. This is a really bad one."

As I came down for my landing, one of the oddest things happened. I wear a cross. The cross itself is one and a half inches long and hangs on a long chain. The necklace swung around my head, and the cross got between my skull and the pavement. As the back of my head bounced off the asphalt, something very sharp embedded itself into the base of my skull. I went down for the count. Blackness swept over me. The world I knew disappeared.

• • •

"I don't see that white light everybody talks about," I said into the air. "Where's that white light?"

I sensed two people or two "somethings" standing on either side of me.

"Am I dead? This is it?" I asked. "I'm done?"

The idea began to grow on me.

"Hey! That wasn't so bad! It could have been a lot worse!"

I thought of illness and cancer. In sudden realization I asked, "That's all she wrote?" Colors swarmed around me, and if truth be told, the two "people" standing next to me reminded me of asterisks.

What struck me so vividly is that I had not turned into something other than what I am. Granted, my physical body lay on the ground, but my spirit was unaltered. What continued to be my personality or the inside of me stayed intact.

I thought back to commitments and decisions I had

made in my life.

"Okay. I'm ready. Let's go," I announced.

I felt a soothing sense of knowledge and peace encompass me. Fear did not exist. Any previous worry of "If anything ever happened to me, how will Ludwig and Pu survive?" left me in the blink of an eye. They would be just fine.

I realized I couldn't "take it with me." Suitcases are not an option. I couldn't even leave with the clothes on my back. My clothes lay in a bloody mess covering my crumpled body with a horse hovering beside it.

I recalled other early, sudden deaths . . . deaths of those who left "before their time," and of the sadness that can engulf those who survive.

"If they only knew!" I wanted to shout.

One of the Asterisks said, "She has to get up."

I sensed anticipation coming from Asterisk Number One.

"I don't want to get up. I'm done," I said.

"No, you're not," replied Asterisk Number One, "You are not 'done.' You have to get up before you do get killed."

Stonebrook and Alfonse searched each other's faces for suggestions.

"She has to make the decision to get up herself," Alfonse reminded Stonebrook. "Everybody has a choice. Free will, you know."

"Well, that doesn't mean we can't try to convince her," Stonebrook insisted.

Asterisk Number One shook me.

"Okay, little lady, rise and shine! Up and at 'em!

Time to get up. You are not done yet. You cannot go yet," he said.

He continued to shake me.

"But I don't want to get up. I'm afraid to get up!" I whimpered. "Can't I just stay here? It's bad, isn't it? This is a bad one. My face is pretty bad, isn't it?"

They looked at each other, wondering what to tell me. "Well, it depends. Hmm. Yes. You will think it is pretty bad," observed Asterisk Number One.

"Hey! I'm not supposed to be talking to you guys!" I remembered.

There was a long pause.

"This is an extenuating circumstance," asserted Asterisk Number One. "You have to get up."

He poked me sharply.

"Quit POKING me! You're kind of stern for an angel. How come I get a stern one?"

Asterisk Number One grimaced. Stonebrook and Alfonse glanced at each other, and Stonebrook rolled his eyes. Alfonse held back a chortle, seeming to communicate, "I'm not going to touch that one."

Asterisk Number One conveyed, "In your case, you need a stern one. Now, open your eyes. You need to get up and go for help."

"I don't want to forget this," I told them. "I want to remember this."

Chapter Thirteen

Amazing Grace

In the distance, I thought I heard my mother calling, "Callie! Time to get up!"

I opened my eyes and saw bright, blue sky above me. Kizzy nestled her muzzle to my chest and sniffed. I raised my head slightly and realized my clothes were blood-soaked.

"Uh, oh," I said.

I half-remembered talking to some people. "Am I dreaming?" I felt surprised that Kizzy just stood there. Animal and Sam observed me from the other side of the locked gate.

"How did I get that gate locked?" I asked Kizzy.

Blood streamed down my face.

"Oh, man," I said. "This is a bad one. I have to get to a mirror."

I really did not want to assess the damage. "Why did this have to happen to me?"

In less than a minute's time, a life is changed. I will not be setting the table for dinner tonight. I sat up carefully, half in a daze, and braced myself with my two hands firm against the asphalt. My hands were gritty, full of little stones.

"I don't think I can get up," I said aloud to Kizzy or anyone listening. "I don't think I can stand. What if I can't walk?"

I grunted my own response. I turned myself over

and supported myself with my hands and knees. I resembled a whipped dog. One arm raised itself, then the other, and I knelt upright in position.

"I think I need some help, Kizzy."

Each arm suddenly felt very light. I detected "air" beneath each arm, and the air helped me to my feet. A fresh breeze brushed my face.

Now standing, I touched the back of my head, and discovered a piece of metal sticking out of my skull.

"The cross?" I thought in shock.

I decided not to pull it out of my skull. Usually it's best to let doctors remove objects from skulls.

I looked down at my legs and checked for broken bones. I had no idea if Kizzy had trampled me during the fall. My legs moved and somewhat dumbfounded, I walked. I put Kizzy back inside the fence, and all three horses appeared calm.

I remembered the approaching storm and looked up into the sky. The storm had vanished. It went north.

I slowly made my way to the house. The perfectionist in me hesitated at the backdoor. I didn't want to make a mess. I stopped at the kitchen sink and let the flowing blood run down the drain. "What if I don't have a face left?" I asked myself. "Well, that would be a kicker, wouldn't it?" I answered myself.

I grabbed a towel off the sink, placed it under my chin, and headed for the bathroom mirror. I did not want to look. I did not want to know if I was deformed.

I glanced into the mirror and gasped. Apparently the metal gate had found its impact right below my eyes.

"At least I can still see," I noted.

I searched further.

"Oh, no!" I cried. "I had such a cute nose!"

I fingered my face, wondering if my cheek bones were also broken, but I really couldn't feel anything at all. My face had swelled and was on numb alert. My skin felt like plastic.

"Get to the Emergency Room," I told myself. "Make a phone call."

I reached for the phonebook, while trying to hold the towel under my chin. In sinking hope, I realized how far we were from help. Ludwig was almost two hours away. Should I drive myself?

Probably not. What if I passed out?

Should I call the police? Is this really an emergency? What exactly does constitute an emergency? I'm alive and I can walk. I'm just missing half my face.

I quickly calculated ambulance costs. Do I really want to spend five-hundred dollars for a ride? Think! Who is at home this time of day?

Maybe Sally's home. Sally is an alternate on the bowling team. I paged through the phonebook for her number.

"Hello?" shouted a huffy, puffy voice.

"Hi, Sally, this is Callie from bowling?"

I told her what had happened.

"I was wondering if you could give me a ride to the hospital?"

"Sure!" she replied, shouting into the receiver. Sally is a "shouter-speaker."

"I can't believe you found me in the house!" she shouted. "I just came in for a glass of water! I'm chopping a cord of wood in the backyard!"

Sally is a hard-working, get up at four-thirty in the morning kind of gal. Sally doesn't believe in paying gas companies. Sally creates her own fuel.

"I'll be right over!" she shouted in my ear. Sally is also a fast driver of cars I soon discovered.

I called Ludwig.

"Ludwig, you'll have to pick up Pu from school today. I had an accident. I'm headed for the hospital. Sam broke my face."

"Oh, Callie! I'll be right home!"

"No. It's okay. Sally from bowling is going to drive me to the hospital. I'll give you a call from there. It's okay, really. I'll be fine. Sally's here! Gotta run!"

Sally spun into the driveway, leapt out of the car, took one look at me, and said, "You really got blasted!"

• • •

Stonebrook and Alfonse looked on. Stonebrook glanced into the air, turned, and informed Alfonse, "Beatrice is on the other end working out details. She needs to know which hospital."

"Callie's deciding right now," Alfonse relayed.

Alfonse strained his ears toward the direction of the car.

"Cedarhills. They're headed for Cedarhills Hospital. It will take them forty minutes to get there."

"Not with Sally driving," Stonebrook told him. "Cedarhills? Do they have a plastic surgeon at Cedarhills?"

Stonebrook snapped his fingers in the air, pulling in

answers. "You go on ahead, Alfonse. I'll stay with the car."

• • •

Sally squealed the car down the driveway, faced me and shouted, "You're sure going to have some black eyes tomorrow!"

I turned my swelling, bloody face toward Sally and wondered if flashing sirens might be more soothing.

"So! What was your bowling average last week? I hit a 180! Do you want some music? Here, I'll turn on the radio!"

We barreled down Highway 30 with Sally honking and flashing her headlights at the cars in front of us, creating our own ambulance run. Cars pulled off to the side of the road. We reached Cedarhills Hospital in twenty-seven minutes flat.

When we barreled into the hospital emergency room, the nurses at the desk took one look at me and began stewing.

One looked up at me and smiled. "Let me take you to a bed, dear. Did you lose consciousness?"

"I'm not sure," I replied. "I was talking to some asterisks, and I have a cross stuck in my head."

I waved goodbye to Sally, and thanked her for the help. "Let me know what happens," she said.

"I will. Thanks, Sally!"

Back at the nurses' desk, nurses Bonnie and Linda went to work.

"Do you think ENT Dr. Muller would still be here?"

Linda asked.

"I don't know," replied Bonnie, "But let's see if we can find him!"

Dr. Garvey, the Emergency Room physician, swung open my hospital cubical curtain, widened his eyes, and said, "Whoa! You really got blasted! Let's get some x-rays!"

He called to Linda, "X-rays, Linda!"

"Already on it," she called back.

Dr. Garvey then began to question me. "Callie, are you married? Do you have a boyfriend?"

What in the world? I didn't think I was "that" attractive. Especially in this condition. It then dawned on me that perhaps he wondered if my husband had popped me one.

"Oh, no," I said, "My husband is at work. Sam did it."

"Sam?" he asked raising his eyebrows.

"Sam, the horse," I clarified.

Dr. Garvey was mollified. "Well, you know we do have to check on these things. What kind of horse is it? I do some riding myself. English? Western?"

Linda interrupted by saying, "X-ray is ready for her."

A young, skinny, kamikaze pilot flew me to X-ray. "Don't you have hallway speed limits?" I gasped.

The X-Ray Department clicked pictures. The gurney pilot whisked me back to ER. Careening me through corridors, he bent his upper torso over the head of the gurney to decrease any possible wind resistance. In midair, he planted his feet against the walls of the corridors for a rudder effect. I spun into the emergency cubicle, X-rays and all.

"You really love your job, don't you?" I asked hi

Dr. Garvey snapped the X-rays into the X-ray reading machine. Dr. Muller burst into the ER, holding a roast beef sandwich and a bag of potato chips. I watched as the two conferred earnestly, pointing at my head.

I overheard Dr. Muller say to Dr. Garvey, "I'm free this afternoon. I'll cancel my tee-time. Want to observe?"

The X-rays displayed a textbook example of a pulverized nose, plus a holy reminder embedded in the base of the skull. Dr. Muller called out to me, "The cross just missed your brain! Good thing you have a thick skull!"

He walked over to me, and said, "I'd give you a bite of my sandwich, but you're going into surgery. Hi, I'm Dr. Muller, ENT. Have you eaten today?"

"Surgery?" I questioned. "Ear, Nose, and Throat?"

I questioned whether or not I wanted an Ear, Nose, and Throat man to put my face back together. Believe me, I have plenty of friends who look at cosmetic surgery as a sport. They shop around, get referrals, and pay through the nose, no pun intended.

"Ah, I don't mean this to sound ungrateful, but don't I need a plastic surgeon?" I asked.

Be strong, I told myself. We're talking about my face here. Be assertive when dealing with medical-facial catastrophes.

Dr. Muller smiled. "Believe it or not, this is your lucky day. I am a plastic surgeon. I do reconstructive surgery all over the world. The only reason I'm here is because my wife forgot to pack me a lunch. It's the first time in fifteen years that I've eaten in the cafeteria."

My swollen eyes widened.

"I only come here once a month for a couple of hours of referrals," he tried to explain.

"Say . . . " I said, realizing an opportunity, "do you think you could do my eyes while you're in there? I think my lids are getting a little saggy. A little nip and tuck?"

He laughed. "I don't think so. It's going to take me about five hours to piece your nose back together. The cross will slip right out. You'll just have a holy head."

He looked at me closely. "Well, maybe the eyes in about ten years."

Linda called out, "Anesthesiology is on their way down, Dr. Muller."

A kind, bubbly Dr. Baker asked, "When was the last time you've eaten? Do you have any allergies? Allergies to any foods? How about eggs?"

"Hmm. Eggs. Yes, I think I do have allergies to eggs. Especially dark, perky ones," I responded.

Dr. Baker was satisfied. The surgery was on.

"The operating room is almost ready, Doctor Muller," said Linda.

Linda turned and whispered to Bonnie, "This all seems so bizarre. Take a look at that X-ray, Bonnie. At that cross stuck in her head."

"Garvey said it actually broke the fall," Bonnie whispered back. "It took the impact off the top half of her skull. Muller's going to take the cross out during surgery. Can you believe Muller's here? The man is tops in his field."

"I know!" Linda said. "I couldn't believe I found him in the cafeteria! He never eats lunch here. He's too cheap."

"Been to church lately?" asked Bonnie.

"No. But I think I'll start," answered Linda.

• • •

Stonebrook and Alfonse sat across from each other in the waiting room, flipping through magazines. Stonebrook read *Popular Mechanics*, and Alfonse, *Good Housekeeping.*

"Hey, Stonebrook, have a pen on you?" asked Alfonse. "I want to copy this recipe."

"Hmm, yes. Here you go. Did someone call her family? And where did Beatrice go?"

"They're on their way," replied Alfonse. "Beatrice is taking a lunch break. How does linguine with cilantro pesto and chicken sound for tonight?"

Stonebrook looked over his magazine and said, "Sounds better than dark, perky eggs."

Chapter Fourteen

Marshmalbw Treats

"Come on, Callie!" yelled Corky. "You gotta see this! Ludwig is starting a fire!"

Our pyromaniac was at it again. Ludwig has a special flame-thrower attached to a propane tank, which he uses to start little campfires. Our campfires don't start out in the "camp" category; they blast into orbit rocketed by fuel injection.

Busy bodies skedaddled through the kitchen. Doors slammed, footsteps shuffled, and cupboard doors banged. Corky and Butch flew out the door with packages of hotdogs in their short, stubby hands.

"Who's got the marshmallows?" yelled Pu.

What a beautiful summer evening! The sun was low in the horizon, and the cornfields glistened in the golden rays. I glanced out the dining room window and watched as Ludwig told everybody to stand back.

My heart gave me a tickle. A heart tickle happens only once in a while, and I wish it happened more often. I am not experiencing heart problems; I believe it is my soul's response to joy. It just doesn't get any better than this.

I watched as five children, ages seven to fourteen, romped and played, intertwined with each other. Age does not matter at Alfalfabit Soup. The older children enjoy the younger ones just as much as the younger ones feel so very privileged to be included in, and part of, the older ones' lives and play.

I had to ask myself how much we actually sacrificed in our move from city to country. I truly do not miss traffic congestion, drive-by shootings and long super-market lines. What I do miss is going to the movies, Chinese take-out, and pizza delivery.

This is not my personal fantasy. It is real. Alfalfabit Soup exists, not as a survey of one-hundred and forty acres, but is made up of the belief and faith held by the people who inhabit it. Alfalfabit Soup is a blessing. Alfalfabit Soup is a gift we are borrowing.

But, as I know, rural life is not paradise in itself. There can also be pain and sorrow. I only need to look or ask. Perhaps it is in the freedom of knowing and realizing what we have or who we are, that we can accept or alter the direction of our lives. Our family chose not only a different lifestyle, but a different life altogether. Growth is often very painful.

"How's your nose, Callie?" asked Constance. "When do you get your bandages off?"

"They're going to pull the nose packing out next week," I replied. "They say it's pretty painful. I've heard horror stories about nose packing."

Constance cringed. "Those horses. Anytime you get a thousand-pound animal losing it . . . "

"Tell me about it . . . ," I said, sarcastically.

Corky burst through the kitchen door again. Corky enjoys being the Wiener Roast Master of Ceremonies.

"We're almost ready, Callie! The fire is getting really hot!"

Constance and I busied ourselves. Constance's husband, Rob, conversed with Ludwig over the fire. They were discussing strategy on post-hole digging and power take-offs. I counted people. Nine. Four adults, five kids, including Pu's friends from school. Sometimes, we have twenty.

We have a party on our hands. Only, we don't consider them "parties" at Alfalfabit Soup, because we have so many visitors. We consider it to be part of the program. In the summer, we put our work aside on weekends so that we can play.

"Thanks for making this wonderful pot of baked beans," I told Constance. "I just love your beans."

Pot luck is an ingenious concept. By this time, my outdoor entertaining methods had a system. For our campfires, we brought out a table from the small pole building to hold all our goodies. Our goodies have to be up on a table because of the five dogs and the rest of the animals.

There is always some type of commotion surrounding our campfires, because cats, dogs, Elmer and Wilbur, and the peacocks also enjoy them. If one accidentally holds a stick up in the air with a wiener on it, you can be sure that Lucky will steal it. He's worse than a junkyard dog.

One of our sources of entertainment is to let Lucky steal a marshmallow. The marshmallow sticks to his beak, and he struts around with a white, puffy, bulbous nose. We call him "Bubble Beak."

Constance and I went out the backdoor laden with bags of chips, hotdog buns and beans. Pu and her friends followed us with marshmallows, graham crackers and chocolate bars for Smores. White plastic yard chairs circled the campfire, and Rob and Ludwig took up fire-pit residency.

"Everybody ready for a stick hunt?" I asked.

All of the children took off for the woods. Constance and I joined them, with the dogs right on our heels. Ludwig and Rob waved to us, while enjoying a moment of silence.

Pu and I had helped Ludwig blaze trails through the woods. The woods are my very favorite part of the farm. We have turned our woods into our own nature pre-serve. I just don't think there is anything more beautiful than a woods filled with towering, one-hundred-year-old maple trees.

I don't even know how tall the trees are, but they seem to reach heaven. The sunlight brushes their flow-ery tops and then filters down to softly illuminate the moss-covered ground. Each leaf holds a different di-mension of green, and if my eyes could only see this once in my lifetime, I would leave happy.

I try to identify each and every tree in the twenty acres of woods. I believe I know them intimately. I have always held a special place in my heart for trees. I revel in the smell of the woods, deeply drinking in the actual difference in oxygen, indulging in its purity.

Pu and I cherish the woods. Our travels throughout the winding paths have come to be known as "The Ad-ventures of Pu and Mom." We pack lunches and delight in our explorations. To the two of us, each and every wildflower, and each tiny bug present themselves as a new creation.

Our mother and daughter "Adventure Lunch" does not take place in front of a television, but rather on top of long grass, flattened by a sleeping deer. We gobble our sandwiches, empty our juice boxes and then lie back on the soft, matted earth, looking up through the tops of the trees into the blue sky. Pu has asked me, "Why do we do all of this stuff, Mom?"

And I have answered with a smile, "So that you can teach your children, Pu. They will need to know that it's okay to take a good risk and that it's all right to be different. An adventure creates an experience. We need to experience life, not just live it."

"But how will I know a good risk from a bad one?" she wanted to know.

"You will know it in your heart, my love."

• • •

"Corky! Pu! Kids! Come here! Quick!" I yelled.

All the children ran over to me, expecting to find a gigantic dinosaur bone. At least a deer antler or two. Perhaps an ancient burial site.

"Take a look at this!" I announced. "Now this is a good one," I said of a tree. "This is a good climber."

The children looked back at me as if I was off my rocker.

I smiled. "Just take a look at this branch! It's offering you a seat!"

Pu's friends glanced at each other, eyeballs rolling, and then Pu's friend, Melanie, asked, "You mean climb it?"

"Of course!"

I would have climbed it myself right then and there, but I reserved this pleasure until tomorrow. There is nothing like sitting in a good tree all by yourself.

I looked around at the faces.

"Haven't you kids climbed trees before?" I asked in astonishment.

They giggled, and then a brave soul informed me, "Isn't that a little dumb?"

Ah, yes, the "World of Plastic."

"The Plastic-World has done you a disservice, my little friends. You don't know what you're missing."

"But won't we get hurt?" asked Melanie.

"Hurt? How's a tree going to hurt you?" I laughed.

"Let me up there!" cried Corky.

Well, needless to say, we spent about an hour taking turns sitting in the tree, as our baked beans got cold.

We emerged from the woods brighter, happier, and more informed tree-people. Ludwig and Rob saw us bobbing up the hill, singing loud, rowdy camp songs off-key and thrusting out our hot dog/marshmallow sticks like knights returning from a conquest. With adhesive bandages plastered across my face, I looked the part.

Our song-singing continued, and grew into who could sing the worst and the loudest. Silliness overcame us, and we giggled and laughed until our sides hurt. If we can't be silly at a campfire, where, indeed, can we be silly?

There's just not enough silliness in this world. Our hotdogs tasted as good as a flame-broiled filet mignon at any four-star restaurant, only to be outdone by the toasted marshmallows. Marshmallow connoisseurs unite.

Corky prefers the "Torch Marshmallow." Lighting it afire in the blue-white flame, the marshmallow is allowed to burn for five seconds before it is blown out and consumed. Corky does not care whether or not the center is done.

Pu, and I, on the other hand, prefer a golden-brown, shiny, toasted gleam to ours, with a slight hardening of an outer crust, gently roasted in glowing embers, to give it the slow-cooked, melted, inner quality we have come to love and adore.

Tummies full to the bursting point, we all sat back and stared at the fire. Elmer and Wilbur plopped down beside us for tummy rubs along with the dogs and cats.

The sun had set and a chill came up in the air. Ludwig put two big logs on the fire to bring up the blaze.

"Callie?" asked Corky in a small voice.

"Yes, Corky?"

"Remember that story about the bull?"

"Sure," I replied. "The one about Marty?"

"Can you tell it to me one more time?"

"Well, sure. If everybody else wants to hear it."

"Yes! Yes!" said Butch eagerly. "I want the bull story!"

I pondered for a moment, and then began, "Once upon a time there was a place called Alfalfabit Soup . . ."

Chapter Fifteen

A Whole Lotta Bull

Just another ordinary day greeted the three of us. We sat at the kitchen table, as we usually do, going over the upcoming day's tasks and events. Pu was driving in with Ludwig to work, as she sometimes does, to spend the day with her dad.

PuLaRoo enjoys these times with her father, and frequently helps Heather, his office manager, insert numbers into the computer. Sometimes he lets Pu talk over the short-wave radio to call in the drivers. No doubt, they will make a special day of it, and meet Ludwig's friend, Beryl, for lunch at the Chinese restaurant down the street.

"Now, don't forget to bring me the leftovers," I reminded them.

I felt tempted to go in and do data entry myself just to get Chinese lunch. I sat back, daydreaming of fresh, crisp egg-rolls and cream-cheese wontons. By George, if this continues, I just may have to become an ethnic cook.

"What are you going to do today, Mom?" asked Pu.

"This morning, the farrier comes to shoe the horses, and this afternoon I'm going to play 'Supply Sergeant'," I told her. "We're out of dog food, pig food, chickenfeed, and milk."

"Gary's funny," Pu said of our farrier, "He always does amazing things."

"Yes," I agreed, "It's not everyone who gets a rodeo clown for a farrier."

People always surprise me. I learned that not only is Gary a rodeo clown, he is also a bull rider. In other words, Gary is no wimp.

I waved goodbye to my little brood, keeping an eye open for Gary's arrival. All the horses were stalled, waiting for him.

I missed Gary's arrival because the phone rang.

"Good morning, Callie, this is your neighbor, Betty, from down the road."

"Morning, Betty, how are you?" I responded.

"Pretty good, Callie, but we were wondering if you have a bull?"

"A bull?" I laughed.

I had to think for a second. What does she mean, do I have a bull? Why, yes, I guess I do have a bull, come to think of it. Does Betty want to borrow our bull? Why would Betty want to borrow our bull? Betty doesn't even have cows.

Betty laughed. "We have a bull in our front yard! It sounds like he's lost."

I laughed, too. A bull in the front yard. That is pretty funny.

"He's staring at me through the kitchen window. The children are terrified," she continued. "Can you hear him bellowing?"

I strained my ear on the receiver end, and what I heard was, "Mom! He's taking off!"

"Well, I wonder whose bull it is," I pondered. "I know it's not our bull because Marty's in the pasture."

"I just thought I'd check with you," said Betty.

We chatted for a few minutes.

"It was the funniest thing!" Betty told me. "I thought it was my husband. I was in the bedroom, and Mike was in the shower. I heard this noise. Sometimes Mike sings in the shower, and I had to laugh. He sounded awful. He sounded like a cow!"

"Betty, this is too funny," I chuckled.

"I was ready to sign him up for singing lessons, but then he came out with a towel wrapped around him. And the kids started screaming downstairs."

Betty demonstrated the bellowing.

I blew coffee out my nose.

"That's not the end of it!" she cried. "We just planted two-hundred tree seedlings in the back yard. He ate them!"

Through my tears of laughter, I glanced out the diningroom window.

"Oh, sorry! Betty, the farrier's here! I have to run!" I told her.

"I have to call around anyway," she said. "Somebody's missing a bull. Now he's headed down Highway 30."

I bolted out the backdoor to meet Gary. With wings on my feet, I paused in midair while making a survey of the pasture. My feet almost missed the ground.

It is amazing my eyes found the hole. But, then, I am extremely farsighted. Ludwig calls me "Eagle Eye."

Our three-rail, two-by-six fence was missing a middle and a top rail. Something had snapped it in two, and that something might be Marty. Marty was nowhere to be seen.

I continued to run toward the barn, stopping short at the door as not to excite the horses. Gary glanced up from his bent position behind a horse.

"Hi, there!" he said.

I could hardly speak.

"Ah . . . ah . . . ah . . ." I said.

"Spit it out," he laughed.

"Ah . . . ah . . . ah . . ." I verbalized.

Just then, I realized my good fortune. Gary could handle this. Gary could lasso Marty just like in the rodeo.

"Gary!" I finally managed, "Our bull is missing!"

"Calm down, now, Callie," he said, "What do you mean your bull is missing?"

"He's at the neighbor's house."

"What's he doing at the neighbor's house?"

In my frustration, I said, "He's having morning coffee. He broke the fence, Gary . . . what am I going to do?"

"Boy, Callie, that's a tough one. What are you going to do?"

Me? I thought. What am I going to do? Gary is going to "do."

"You . . . you . . . can catch him, can't you?" I asked.

"Me? Oh, no. I can't catch him," he replied.

"What?" I asked in shock. "You can't catch him?"

"You don't 'catch' a bull, Callie. That's a two-thousand pound animal with a mind of his own."

"But you do it all the time!"

"Inside a ring, Callie. In a controlled environment. Bulls can be very dangerous."

I stood there, at a loss for words. My mind began to race in panic. I thought of Marty headed down Highway 30. If a car hit him, we would be liable. I thought not for money, but for potential injuries.

"Let me tell you just how dangerous these bulls are, Callie," Gary continued. "I lost one of my best friends because of a bull. Chip was stock-trailering a bull to market. He went inside the trailer to unlock the dividing gate. The bull went nuts and crushed him against the wall. He literally stepped on his head."

Gary raised his eyebrows at me, expecting I'd get the picture.

"They're totally unreliable. You never know when their mind is going to switch over to charge. No. I can't go catch him. Neither can you."

Overwhelmed, I thought of Marty terrifying the countryside.

"What can I do?" I asked in shock.

"I can shoot him," he responded. "I have a rifle in the truck."

"Oh, boy," I said, "I don't think Ludwig is going to like that."

"You don't have a choice, Callie."

Yes, what choice did I have?

"Do you think you're going to throw a halter and a lead rope on him?" he asked, sarcastically.

"Gary," I said, "I have to try. I'm going to try."

"What?!"

"There's no telling how much damage he's doing out there. I'm going to go find him. I can't let him hurt someone."

"Callie. I can bring him down in two shots."

"I have to try."

Had I lost my mind? Perhaps.

"And how in God's name are you going to catch him?" he asked.

Oh, yes! "That's it!" it dawned on me. "In God's name," I said aloud. I will try IN God's name.

"Gary, I'm going to ask God to help me," I told him bluntly.

"Well, I sure hope He listens to you more than He does me," he said, skeptically. "You're walking to your death, Callie. I'll order your tombstone."

"A bucket of grain," I blurted. "I need a bucket of grain. And yes, a scoop."

"You think you're going to catch him with a bucket of grain?" he asked.

"Want to come with me?" I asked, still hopeful.

"No, Callie. I do not want to go with you. I do not want to watch you die. I'm serious."

I got in our pickup truck, barely able to start it. My hands shook, and I tried to focus on our long driveway, hoping not to run off the road. Highway 30 is about two miles away.

I stopped the truck halfway down the driveway. I gripped the steering wheel and shouted very much aloud, "THIS IS AN EMERGENCY! THIS IS AN EMERGENCY, GOD! I HOPE YOU CAN HEAR ME!"

I hoped my guardian angels had not stopped for morning coffee at the Plugged Artery. My grip on the steering wheel loosened, and I made my way down the driveway and over to Highway 30. I rotated my head, sweeping my eyes from left to right over the horizon while keeping a centered position on the road.

I noticed a truck with a load of corn behind it, pulled off to the side of the road. A seasoned farmer dressed in Carhartt bib overalls waved at me, and I pulled over.

"He's up in the alfalfa field," he told me, pointing in Marty's direction.

"Can you help me?" I asked, wistfully.

"Sorry," he said, sounding very sorry, "It's too dangerous."

I thanked him for stopping. Marty grazed in the alfalfa field about four-hundred feet away. "Good luck!" he yelled, as he drove off.

Too bad I couldn't just leave Marty in the alfalfa field. He looked mighty happy. I grabbed the scoop and filled it with grain. I walked slowly away from the truck some thirty feet, stood in the alfalfa field, waved my hands and called out, "Yoo Hoo!"

Marty looked up from grazing and appeared very startled. Uh, oh, I thought. Marty's going to run away. Marty is going to charge.

In sudden panic, I thought, what if this isn't our bull? How do I know it's Marty out there? How many bulls are lost in alfalfa fields today? It must be Marty!

"Marty! It's Mom!" I yelled.

Marty's dumbfounded expression turned to recognition. Like, "Why, it's Mom! Mom found me!"

"Marty!" I called again.

Oh, dear. Marty muscled his energy and actually began to leap into the air. I looked back at the truck, wondering what to do next. Marty continued to bound, this way and that, bouncing in my direction. I tried to calculate how fast he could bounce.

Marty put on the brakes and slid to a stop, ten feet away from me. I closed my eyes and prepared for the worst. I wasn't dead, so I peeked. If I didn't know better, I could practically imagine an invisible wall between the two of us.

Marty stared at me and our eyes met. Frantically, I wondered if I should look away. Does this mean I am challenging a bull, or he me? I remembered, "I'm the mom. Moms do not look away."

Marty broke the gaze first and bent his head to the ground. He swung his head around and around and snorted, flinging mucous all over the place. Yikes, I thought. Is this a prelude to a charge?

"He's going to charge me, God!" I yelled into my mind.

I suddenly wanted a cape. But then, I didn't know what to do with a cape in the first place. Oh, my word, am I wearing any red? What does the color red mean, anyway?

Marty was too close for me to start running to the truck. I lifted up my hand which was holding the scoop. I shook the scoop so that the grain rustled enticingly.

"Marty," I said firmly, "Dinner. Marty, dinner."

Marty took his head off the ground, but continued to shake it and snort through his nose. He began to walk toward me. I held out my little scoop.

"That's a good boy," I told him. "Dinner."

Marty started to eat the grain out of the scoop. His head was so massive it dwarfed the scoop, and he had to use his tongue to reach the grain. A scoop of grain only goes so far, and I realized it would be gone oh so soon.

I walked backwards to the truck. My hand reached behind for the door handle. Marty wanted more grain.

I slipped inside the truck and had no idea what to do next. I couldn't exactly walk him home. Or could I? I rolled down the window and talked to him.

I looked over on the seat at the bucket of grain. I put more grain into the scoop. I reached my arm out the window and offered him the scoop. He took a bite, I started the truck, and I hoped it wouldn't scare him.

The wheels of the truck moved, and Marty seemed to say, "Hey, where are you going?"

I needed to turn the truck around in order to change directions. Cars traveled by us, glancing in our direction, but now I had to take up the whole highway with my illegal U-turn and a bull. The coast was clear. With my hand held out the window, I made my turn, and Marty followed, taking up the center of the highway.

I was forced to make a decision on which lane to plug. The road shoulder was barely existent. I chose driving in the wrong lane, going the opposite direction, because fields adjoined that side of the road rather than driveways or houses. I didn't want Marty to get sidetracked.

I put on my hazard lights and hoped people would see me.

Let's just say they did not miss the bull walking down the highway at them. I looked like Little Bo Peep driving a truck.

Consistent with my middle name, "Worry," I worried whether or not this lent itself to a traffic ticket. A highway patrolman seemed welcome at this point. No one stopped to give me a ticket. They just stared. Lunch fodder at the Plugged Artery, here we come.

Marty and I made our way home. To my amazement, Marty followed at the same distance and did not deviate five feet away from the truck. He walked and sometimes bounced alongside.

I felt "angel assisted." It felt as if I had angels walking along beside me. Angels between Marty and myself, and angels on the other side of Marty directing him. Each and every step Marty took appeared orchestrated.

We reached our long driveway, and I pulled in from the road wiping the sweat off my brow. Thirteen hundred feet to go. At least we were in safe territory. Or so I thought.

Marty followed me up the driveway, recognized the property, and went a little ahead of the truck. I could see Gary standing in the open barn door with his hands over his eyes to shade the sun.

At this point, I had another problem. I couldn't exactly drive Marty through the gate into the pasture. That particular gate was only four feet wide. Right before we reached the barn, I stopped the truck. I turned the motor off, took my grain scoop and got out.

"As I live and breathe," gasped Gary.

I glanced at Gary, not knowing whether to smile, laugh, or pass out. I tried to keep my eyes on Marty.

"I will remember this the rest of my life," Gary said, making a "whew" sound.

Marty looked at Gary and thought it might be nice to join him in the barn.

"Uh oh," said Gary.

"Marty, over here. Dinner," I said shaking the scoop.

One-hundred-and-fifty-feet to the pasture gate seemed impossible. I had to walk it without the protection of the truck. If Marty made one quick move or even decided to nudge me, I could be dead. I closed my eyes.

Faith. Faith, I told myself. I have to have faith. I've come this far. I remembered one of my favorite scripture passages, "I tell you the truth, if you have faith as small as a mustard seed, you can say to this mountain, 'Move from here to there' and it will move. Nothing will be impossible for you." Matthew 17:20,21

I could certainly relate to the mustard seed. I felt as if I was about two inches tall. My mountain stood before me. Mountains can come in various sizes and shapes. Mine weighed two thousand pounds.

"Come on, Marty. Let's go. Let's go home," I said.

I stuck out my scoop, and he walked beside me. He waited for me while I unlatched the gate. I walked through the gate ahead of him and put the scoop down on the ground. I climbed over the fence. Marty looked up from the scoop, spotted the girls in the distance, and snorted.

I heard a voice behind me.

"How did you do that?" Gary whispered.

I turned, looked at Gary and smiled.

"Oh, my word," he continued to whisper. "How, Callie?"

"Faith, Gary," I answered. "You have to have a little

faith."

• • •

Word did reach the Plugged Artery. On Friday, at eleven-thirty I met Constance for lunch. I walked in the door and searched the tables for Constance. Constance waved to me from a booth in the back.

Per usual, the center of the restaurant contained a long, connecting table. This is where farmers sit along with feed-store employees. Every day they have lunch and shoot the breeze.

The long table came to a hush as I walked through the restaurant. Chuck, Earl, Floyd, Marvin, and Leroy looked up at me as I angled myself past their jutting chairs.

Now, what? I thought. Oh dear, what did the new-comer do now?

I reached Constance and slid into the booth. The "boys" continued to eye me. Marvin and Leroy gave me the farmer nod. Chuck got out of his seat and ambled toward me.

"Way to go, Callie," he smiled. "We heard about your bull. I want to give you something."

Chuck reached up to his head and pulled off his worn, torn, Carhartt cap. He placed it on top of my head and gave it a tap for good measure.

"Callie," he said smiling, "you're one of us now. Welcome to farming."

I smiled. "Thanks, guys. I'm glad to be here."

Acknowledgments

I wish to thank all those who assisted us in our first year of "farming." It seemed that every single day someone reached out their hand in a helpful way.

Although this book is fiction, most of the animal escapades actually happened. I really did chase Marty down the highway with a scoop of grain. Lucky, the peacock, really did tap on the window and took up residency in the pickup truck. Penny Pig ran away from home. I was kicked in the face by a horse, and my cross necklace was stuck in my head. I believe the cross saved my life. And Elmer and Wilbur, bless their hearts, gave us hours upon hours of enjoyment and laughter. Truth is always stranger than fiction.

Special thanks to "Ludwig and Pu" for being my family! To my parents who didn't know what they started with the plastic cowgirl vest. To Betty Wasiloff who constantly encouraged me through the writing of *Alfalfabit Soup*. We did it, Betty! To Chambers Publishing Group! To Dr. Dean Peterson and his wife, Patty, who inspired the nativity scene story. To our friend Andrea who delightfully schooled us on horses. To my dear friends who were the "test pilots" and/or helpers in *Alfalfabit Soup*; Winn, PR, Sols, Margie, Dan, Ken, Charity, Lois, Roy and Diane! And thank you most of all to my best friend "upstairs" who keeps such a good eye on us.

Permissions

United Parcel Service, used by permission

Carhartt, used by permission

Northwest Airlines, used by permission

Scripture taken from the **HOLY BIBLE, NEW INTERNA-TIONAL VERSION**, Copyright 1973, 1978, 1984 by International Bible Society, Used by permission of Zondervan Publishing House, All Rights Reserved.